POSITIVE PSYCHOLOGY NEWS SERIES

Character Strengths Matter

How to Live a Full Life

Edited by Shannon Polly, MAPP and
Kathryn Britton, MAPP

In Loving Memory

This book is dedicated to the memory of Christopher Peterson (1950-2012), our mentor and inspiration in the exploration of character strengths. Christopher Peterson was the Arthur F. Thurnau professor of psychology at the University of Michigan in Ann Arbor. He was science director of the VIA Institute on Character and co-author of *Character Strengths and Virtues: A Handbook and Classification*. One of the founders of positive psychology, he is noted for his study of character, optimism, health, and well-being. His other books include *A Primer in Positive Psychology* and *Pursuing the Good Life*. In 2010, Dr. Peterson won the Golden Apple Award for outstanding teaching at the University of Michigan.

Acclaim for *Character Strengths Matter*

"My friend, Chris Peterson, would have loved this book. It brings to life with personal stories, practical recommendations, wisdom, and humor the dry scholarship that he (with an assist from me) did in *Character Strengths and Virtues*. Chris was very down-to-earth and I am sure he would have concurred in my enthusiastically recommending this book to everyone who works with character strengths in the real world."

~ Martin E. P. Seligman, author of *Authentic Happiness* and *Flourish*.

"I wish Christopher Peterson were alive to read this book. He would have been proud and grateful. This wonderful book beautifully weaves together art and science, reason and passion, theory and practice—and the outcome is an accessible and rigorous guide that can help us fulfill our potential for success and happiness. It brings Peterson's work on strengths to life!"

~ Dr. Tal Ben-Shahar, author of *Happier, The Pursuit of Perfect,* and *Choose the Life You Want*

"This is what is so stunning about this book: it's the best experiential or *applied* introduction to the psychology of human strengths that I've seen. I learned from this book by *performing* it, not just reading it. This tiny volume has magic in it."

~ Dr. David L. Cooperrider, Case Western Reserve University, The David L. Cooperrider Center for Appreciative Inquiry at Champlain College

"This is an extraordinary book—extraordinary in that it includes the latest research on character strengths but goes well beyond that. It provides five practice guidelines applicable to each strength, and, importantly, provides examples, monologues, poems, and speeches that realistically illustrate each strength. Polly and Britton have provided a tremendous service to the field of positive psychology and positive education by combining scholarship, practice, and illustrations in a way that has not appeared heretofore. I highly recommend this book."

~ Dr. Kim Cameron, William Russell Kelly Professor of Management and Organizations, University of Michigan, author of *Positive Leadership* and *Developing Management Skills.*

"Professor Chris Peterson's monumental contribution to the field of positive psychology lives on in this unique and moving volume on character strengths."
~ Dr. Barbara Fredrickson, University of North Carolina at Chapel Hill, author of *Positivity* and *Love 2.0*

"Character Strengths Matter is best viewed as a gift. It represents the gift Chris Peterson gave to the world with his groundbreaking research on character. It represents the many people who follow in his footsteps by being good stewards of his work and disseminating it widely to those who may benefit. The book's contents reveal an opportunity for all readers to give themselves the gift of character strengths by understanding, exploring, embodying, and expressing their best qualities to improve themselves AND to help others."
~ Dr. Ryan M. Niemiec, education director of the VIA Institute on Character and author of *Mindfulness and Character Strengths*

"This wonderful book is testament to Chris Peterson's legacy of bringing character strengths to life. Through scientific insight, practical advice, and inspirational examples, Britton and Polly engage a whole new audience in living a full life through their character strengths."
~ Dr. Alex Linley, CEO of CAPP and author of *The Strengths Book* and *Average to A+*

"Chris Peterson was one of my favorite people in the whole world, and I had great respect for him as a scientist! This volume is a wonderful tribute to Chris and his work, which I consider to be some of the very best scholarship in positive psychology. Indeed, his research is some of the best research in all of psychology during the past several decades! In terms of virtues, Chris was fair and kind, curious and inquisitive, and funny and fun. We continue to miss Chris a lot, but this book will help us keep him close."

~ Dr. Ed Diener, Senior scientist for the Gallup Organization and author of *Happiness: Unlocking the Mysteries of Psychological Wealth*

"This book is all about living the 'full life' but every page is also full of life! It provides a creative, playful, personal and practical guide on how to apply strengths to everyday situations. To put it simply this book is thoroughly engaging and heart-warming and aptly echoes the fine qualities of our dearly missed Chris Peterson."

~ Dr. Dianne Vella-Brodrick, Director, Master of Applied Positive Psychology program, University of Melbourne

"Chris Peterson was widely regarded as a leader in positive psychology research. This volume is evidence of his profound and positive influence. Here, you will find interviews and articles with people affected by Chris' work on character strengths as well as practical suggestions for using your own. A true testament to his legacy."

~ Dr. Robert Biswas-Diener, author of *The Courage Quotient* and *Happiness: Unlocking the Mysteries of Psychological Wealth*

"Talk to your children about their weaknesses and watch them shrink. Point to their strengths and watch them come alive and, literally, rise to their full height. Though weaknesses need recognition they rarely provide meaningful guidance, and never purpose. Among Christopher Peterson's many strengths, indeed his greatest may have been his ability to help humanity understand its own. In this fine book, combining first-hand insight, practical wisdom, and excellent journalism, Britton and Polly open another fascinating path to Peterson's work, taking it even further. "

~ Dr. Hans Henrik Knoop, Aarhus University,
Past President, European Network for Positive Psychology

"The notion of 'full' in the title is aptly applied to this book, which is full of rich and practical examples of how people can live in strength-based ways. This book is a valuable guide to teachers in secondary school who want to find ways to help their students cultivate character and is also a wonderful book for any person who wants to live a full life. I was particularly attracted to the way this book combines science and 'the arts' to explore character strengths. Such an approach ensures that varied learning styles are catered for and, personally speaking, it appealed to my own signature strength of 'appreciation of beauty and excellence.' Simply put, this is a beautiful book and an excellent tribute to Chris Peterson."

~ Dr. Lea Waters, Expert on strengths-based parenting,
Melbourne Graduate School of Education

"More than any other work to date, Character Strengths Matter honors and embraces the depth and breadth of Chris' contributions. Britton and Polly understand that the applications of the VIA classification extend far beyond the silos of positive psychology and the study of character. The 24 strengths provide a powerful tool for revealing, on the one hand, the essence of our shared humanity, and, on the other, the uniqueness of each individual. The rich combination of research and theory with engaging personal narrative and practical advice can only be described as Petersonesque."

~ Mark Linkins, Positive Education Consultant

"Britton and Polly have put together an engaging and thoughtful book that explores the concept of Character Strengths in a way not yet seen before. The aim of this book is to bring awareness to, exploration of and active engagement with Character Strength and Virtues, and this is achieved in a way that will offer something for everyone. From snippets of literature to excerpts of speeches by Nobel Prize winners, this book is a delight to read and is sure to become recommended reading for all those new and old to positive psychology."

~ Dr. Kate Hefferon, CPsychol, Senior Lecturer of the Masters of Applied Positive Psychology program, University of East London and author of *The Body and Positive Psychology*

"This clarification of Chris Peterson's 24 strengths is charming, rewarding, and a page turner! Nothing else written about the 24 strengths share these three virtues. All students of character and all students of positive psychology should read this wonderful book from cover to cover."

~ George Eman Vaillant, MD, 35-year director of Harvard's Study of Adult Development, author of *Spiritual Evolution*, *Aging Well*, and *Adaptation to Life*.

"A unique collection of cutting-edge research and practical applications for coaches, consultants and educators aiming to help their clients become happier and more productive. All proceeds are being donated to a scholarship to support future researchers—a win-win."

~ Dr. Adam Grant, Wharton professor and *New York Times* bestselling author of *Give and Take*

"This is among the best books in all of positive psychology. It takes one of the most important areas of research — the character strengths — and makes it as accessible, as practical, and as inspiring as could be. I particularly love that it is written for sharing. Every couple and every family should have a copy. This will become my standard dinner party gift, instead of a bottle of wine."

~ Dr. Jonathan Haidt, New York University, author of *The Righteous Mind* and *The Happiness Hypothesis*

POSITIVE PSYCHOLOGY NEWS SERIES

Character Strengths Matter

How to Live a Full Life

Edited by Shannon Polly, MAPP &

Kathryn Britton, MAPP

Series Editor: Senia Maymin, PhD, MAPP

Positive Psychology News, LLC

2015

POSITIVE PSYCHOLOGY
— NEWS DAILY —

Positive Psychology News Daily
http://PositivePsychologyNews.com

Christopher Peterson Memorial Fellowship:
http://bit.ly/CharStrengthsDonation

ISBN: **0692465642**
EAN-13: **978-0692465646**
Internal illustrations by Kevin Gillespie
Cover designed by Haresh R. Makwana

Printed in the United States of America

Table of Contents

List of Figures

Illustrations by Kevin Gillespie

Contributors

Scott Asalone (Using Strengths Assessments in Business)

Diana Boufford (Spirituality)

Kathryn Britton (Interviewed Todd Kashdan on Curiosity; Humility; Prudence)

Aren Cohen (Social Intelligence; Strengths on Vacations)

Kirsten Cronlund (Love and Be Loved)

Paula Davis-Laack (Zest)

Sean Doyle (Fairness)

Elizabeth Elizardi (Character Strengths in Young Children)

Sherri Fisher (Appreciation of Beauty and Excellence)

Margaret Greenberg (Interviewed Tom Rath on Leadership)

Bridget Grenville-Cleave (Kindness)

Tom Heffner (Creativity)

Louisa Jewell (Forgiveness)

Homaira Kabir (Humor)

Sandy Lewis (Open-mindedness)

Neal Mayerson (Foreword; Complex Character Strengths)

Ryan Niemiec (Love of Learning; Signature Strengths)

Shannon Polly (Acting "As If"; Gratitude; Teamwork)

Tayyab Rashid (Five Actions to Build for each strength)

Lisa Sansom (Interviewed Robert Biswas-Diener on Bravery)

Jan Stanley (Integrity)

Yee-Ming Tan (Character Strengths in Business)

Prakriti Tandon (Forgiveness)

Dan Tomasulo (Perspective)

Doug Turner (Hope)

George Vaillant (Love and Be Loved)

Emily vanSonnenberg (Self-regulation)

John Yeager (Character Strengths of High-Risk Youth)

Emiliya Zhivotovskaya (Persistence)

Christopher Peterson

Dedication

This book is dedicated to the memory of Christopher Peterson, a pioneer in the study of character strengths, a mentor for students of character, an exemplar of humor, humility, love, and kindness, and a good friend.

May the seeds you planted continue to grow and prosper.

Shannon and Kathryn

Proceeds from the sale of this book will benefit the Christopher Peterson Memorial Fellowship at the University of Pennsylvania. This fellowship supports the development of practitioners of positive psychology.
http://bit.ly/CharStrengthsDonation

Books in the Positive Psychology News Series

POSITIVE PSYCHOLOGY
—— NEWS DAILY ——

Resilience: How to Navigate Life's Curves
(*http://tinyurl.com/ResilienceBook*)

Gratitude: How to Appreciate Life's Gifts
(*http://tinyurl.com/GratitudeBook*)

Character Strengths Matter: How to Live a Full Life
(*http://bit.ly/CharStrengthsBook*)

Foreword

In 1999, Marty Seligman, then President of the American Psychological Association, and I, then President of the Mayerson Family Foundations, decided to collaborate on a dedicated and focused effort to advance the science and practice of character. Dr. Seligman was at the time conceiving of what he termed a "positive psychology" – one that focused on the positive end of the continuum of human experience. Until then, social sciences focused time, talent, and resources on understanding and ameliorating human suffering. Seligman thought it was time to better understand the making of "a good life" as articulated by Aristotle over two thousand years ago. Seligman envisioned this new sub-discipline as understanding three essential components: positive emotions, positive personality traits, and positive organizations. He characterized positive personality traits as *the backbone* of positive psychology.

As a practicing clinical psychologist at the time, I had spent many years sitting in my office with people with various diagnoses trying to help them move past the problems they presented. I learned much in the course of this work about myself and others. Of the lessons learned, I discovered I was able to help people become unstuck and move forward by focusing on what was right and strong in them as opposed to dwelling too long on what was weak and needed to be fixed. Once I was able to help clients see their positive strengths, this perspective seemed to become a launching pad for more adaptive choices. When we focused on what was wrong with them, their body language would reflect demoralization and often resistance. But when we focused on their strengths of character, they seemed to sit up straighter, their eyes seemed to come alive, and their voices were energized. Because of my experience for many years as a psychotherapist, I felt confident that it was important to launch this effort to

1

advance the science and practice of what's best about human beings, that is, the science of character.

This new challenge had two primary components. First, we had to determine a process for creating what we wanted to be an unprecedented effort. Second, we needed to recruit top talent.

Regarding the first requirement, we hosted a retreat in Glasbern, Pennsylvania, with an eclectic mix of renowned scholars from various fields including biology, philosophy, education, social science, and leaders in the development of the DSM psychiatric manual. We brought them together with positive youth practitioners who ran nationally recognized programs for youth. We wanted the academics to be grounded in the practical. Seligman anticipated that this process would take about 3 years and $1,000,000 in order to ensure the work would have the depth, magnitude, and pedigree that we thought was important for it to become what Harvard professor Howard Gardner later referred to as, "one of the most important initiatives in psychology of the past half century." Envisioning that this work could make an important contribution to the world, I agreed to provide the funding and to lend whatever other resources of networking and experience I could.

Regarding the second requirement, we needed to engage a project director par excellence. When I asked Marty, "Who would be the best person in the world to help us with this substantial project?" without a moment's hesitation he said "Chris Peterson." He warned me that it might be hard to recruit Dr. Peterson since he was a tenured faculty at the University of Michigan with a very active and productive academic life of teaching, researching, and publishing. Additionally, even if he were interested, it would be unusual for his university to allow him to be absent from his responsibilities for 3 years! Nonetheless, I requested that Marty contact Chris and, if he was interested, we could then try to negotiate with the university. As I recall, Marty contacted Chris who expressed some degree of mid-career lull and excitement to take on this new challenge. Through conversations with the University of Michigan, I was able to arrange for Chris to spend 100% of his time for three years on this "science of character" project, paying his salary for two years. The third year was his university sabbatical.

With our core team assembled, and the recognition that understanding human character was a long-term proposition, we created a non-profit organization to be the home and steward of this work for years to come. Originally established as the *Values In Action Institute* - now the *VIA Institute on Character* (i.e., "VIA") – the nonprofit set its mission as "the advancement of the science and practice of character strengths." The immediate goal was to develop the basic tools any new science would need – an intellectual foundation, a nomenclature of key variables for inquiry, and tools for measuring these key variables. After contracting with Drs. Seligman and Peterson, VIA contracted with a variety of character strength experts. In 2004, after three years of hard work involving 55 renowned scholars and practitioners, these tools were created and published. *Character Strengths and Virtues: A Handbook and Classification* presented the intellectual foundation, measurement strategies, and organizing framework that is the *VIA Classification of Character Strengths and Virtues*. The classification identifies 24 strengths of character that are nested under six higher order categories called virtues. At the same time, VIA published initial versions of the VIA Surveys: the VIA Youth and the VIA-IS (for adults).

For the past decade, the *Mayerson Foundation* has further supported the *VIA Institute* in offering the *VIA Survey* for free as well as supporting its efforts to keep both the practice and the science moving along. Over three million people from every country in the world have taken the *VIA Survey*, resulting in the largest database in the world on character strengths. Hundreds of scientific papers have been published in professional journals. Counselors and coaches, educators, organizational development consultants, military personnel, and individuals pursuing personal growth have been finding productive ways to apply character strengths in their respective domains of activity.

The *VIA* work resonates deeply and broadly. We recognize the brilliance of Drs. Peterson and Seligman in creating the foundation of this work. Dr. Peterson was a kind, gentle, funny, and brilliant man. The world owes a debt of gratitude to him and Dr. Seligman for their vision and insights, and for their courage of character for taking on such a monumental challenge. The insights that have been emerging, and the ones yet to come, would not have happened but for these two giants. They, along with the VIA Institute, set out to help humanity pivot towards its better nature, and the momentum has been building. Character strengths matter. Through scientific study, our understanding can be put towards building a better world.

It is befitting that all proceeds from the sale of this book go to the Christopher Peterson Memorial Fellowship at the University of Pennsylvania to help students needing support to attend the Master of Applied Positive Psychology program that Dr. Peterson helped to found. I am honored to have been asked to write the foreword to this collection of papers. I am also grateful and humbled by my character strength journey that continually awes me with pleasant surprises and connects me with kindred spirits. Thank you to all who are grabbing hold of this early stage work and running with it. It takes many people linking arms with one another to accomplish great things. The best is yet to come.

Neal H. Mayerson, Ph.D.,
Chairman, VIA Institute on Character
February 15, 2015

Introduction

How can you live a full life? A key step is to leverage your character strengths in service of yourself, your family, your workplace, your community, and your world.

Your first question may be, "What are character strengths?"

Borrowing from the words of Christopher Peterson in *A Primer on Positive Psychology*, we need "a vocabulary for speaking about the good life and an assessment strategy for investigating its components." Character strengths are the components of the good life. These are qualities valued across time, across nationalities, and across religions as the elements of strong and virtuous behavior. They are qualities that we value in ourselves, our friends, our children, our colleagues, and our leaders.

In order to build the list of twenty-four elementary character strengths described in this book, Christopher Peterson led a team of experts that first settled on 10 criteria for inclusion and then sifted through candidate qualities drawn from literature, religious writing, psychology, and many other fields. Neal Mayerson describes the process in the Foreword. In particular, they were looking for a relatively small number of elementary strengths that cannot be broken down into combinations of other strengths. In a particular individual, these elementary strengths work together to form more complex character strengths, as Neal Mayerson describes at the end of Part 1.

Each individual has a particular configuration of the 24 character strengths, some overused, some underused, and some used in just the right amount. The strengths that most characterize a particular individual are sometimes called his or her signature strengths. Ryan Niemiec describes signature strengths in the last chapter in the book.

Your second question might then be, "Why do character strengths matter?" When people are aware of their own character strengths, they use them more intentionally for their own benefit and for the benefit of the people around them. There is, for example, a well-studied exercise for improving well-being that involves using one's signature strengths in novel ways. In the last chapter, Ryan Niemiec sketches some of the research that tracks the beneficial impact of this exercise in a variety of environments. Awareness of character strengths leads to greater energy and involvement in school, family, and work. Learning how to recognize and reflect back other people's strengths makes us better parents, teachers, bosses, friends, and mentors. Having a language to talk about character strengths makes us more aware of what is strong and worth nourishing in each other.

Finally, you might ask, "How do I grow my own character strengths and the strengths of my children, colleagues, and friends?" Ryan Niemiec, an expert on character strengths development, has developed a process with 3 steps:

Become _aware_ of your existing character strengths by taking the online Values in Action survey at *http://bit.ly/VIASurvey*. It will give you a list of the twenty-four VIA strengths in rank order from the strength you express the most to the one you express the least. You will be joining over three million people from around the world who have already taken the VIA survey.

Second _explore_ the strengths that interest you, especially the ones that are your signature strengths, the ones that you apply most naturally in multiple settings and that bring you most energy. You could also explore other strengths, such as ones at the bottom of your list. Sometimes there is benefit in investing time developing a strength that does not come as easily to you. Think about ways that you already use your strengths, as well as ways you might be overusing or underusing them.

Third, _take action_ to use your strengths mindfully as you work toward goals or solve problems in your life.

This is a book to help you explore and take action.

Use Part 1 to explore. It contains a chapter for each of the twenty-four character strengths arranged alphabetically for easy reference. Each chapter has the same basic structure: a definition of the character strength, articles showing how the character strength shows up in daily life, a list of ways to build the strength, and finally a passage to read aloud to help you embody the character strength. See the Part 1 introduction for more information about the structure of each chapter.

Use Part 2 to think about ways to take action. Part 2 shows applications of character strength knowledge in different contexts: with small children, with disadvantaged youth, in business settings, even on vacations. It also includes an article defining signature strengths and offering several clear tips for putting signature strengths into practice.

This book doesn't have to be read from cover to cover. You could pick it up to explore your top character strength or go right to one that you want to work on. You could read it as a survey to get a general sense of character strengths in action. You could read Part 2 to investigate ways to put knowledge of character strengths to work and then turn to Part 1 to explore individual strengths in detail.

In Parts 1 and 2, you can hear the perspectives of more than 50 people, including authors of the articles and authors of the poems and plays and speeches to be read aloud.

This book contains a wealth of information about character strengths: definitions, stories, reflections, suggestions, and finally passages for you to read aloud to help you embody each strength. Yes, reading aloud is a way to build character strengths. Curious? Read on.

Acting "As If"

by Shannon Polly

Children play. They imagine. They play 'dress up'. Right now my two- and four-year-olds are crawling around the house pretending to be a lion and a baby on their way to their castle. It is by playing 'mommy' or 'doctor' or 'dragon-slayer' that they try new things and learn how to grow into adulthood.

But something happens when people get older. They get put in boxes. You are a teacher, and teachers only do certain things. You are a businesswoman, so you can't also be a ballroom dancer.

To explore what happens when we jump to conclusions, I facilitate a game called "Two truths and a lie," in some of my workshops. When I tell participants that I was an actor and an associate Broadway producer, they think it's the lie. "But you couldn't be," they respond. "You're the facilitator!" Society tells us how to fit into our roles so that we become more easily categorized. But this limits our creativity and our development.

The truth is that we play many characters in our lives. I am a mother, a wife, a daughter, a businesswoman, and a friend.

Shakespeare put it best in *As You Like It:*
> *"All the world's a stage,*
> *And all the men and women merely players;*
> *They have their exits and their entrances,*
> *And one man in his time plays many parts."*

So how do we break out of being stuck in particular roles? Both acting teachers, like Konstantin Stanislavsky, and psychologists, like Alfred Adler, recognized the benefits of taking on new roles for development.

According to Adler, "When people have difficulty [...] speaking assertively or responding with some measure of empathy, the clinician might encourage them to act "as if" they were assertive or empathic several times a day until the next session. As people begin to act differently and to feel differently, they become different."

To apply the actor's tool kit to real life, we can act "as if" with our intentions, emotions, and physicality. One excellent way to act "as if" is to read aloud.

Social psychologist Daryl Bem states that humans form conclusions about themselves by observing themselves in the same way that they form conclusions about others by observing them. Acting "as if" gives people opportunities to enact best possible outcomes or to create new stories about their lives. Asking people to pretend can help them get past resistance to change because it is temporary and merely an experiment.

At the same time, acting "as if" can also feel risky. No one wants to look silly in front of his or her peers. I've had coaching mentors tell me *not* to use the term 'role play' because clients have such visceral negative reactions to the idea of performing. But when I ask clients to "try on" that conversation with their boss about reducing hours, the words flow, and the future conversation becomes less daunting. The fear of the conversation turns out to be worse than the conversation itself. So what are we doing when we "try on" that conversation?

In human development, we venture from who we are right now into who we are not yet but could be, territory that Russian psychologist Lev Vygotsky called our *zone of proximal development* (ZPD). The acquisition of new knowledge is dependent on previous learning as well "trying on" new behaviors, often reflected back to us by the people around us. If a baby says "ba-ba," we don't say "Nope, that's not it. Try again!" We say, "Bottle! Look honey, she just said 'bottle'!" As adults we help children grow into what they can become. When you finish words for babies, they are growing in their ZPDs. When we "try on" new ways of behaving, we are venturing into our own ZPDs and expanding our ideas about what is possible.

When I facilitate workshops on character strengths, I find that many people immediately focus on the strengths at the bottom of their personal rankings. We are hardwired with a negativity bias, and our culture perpetuates the myth that our greatest room for growth is in our areas of weakness. I frequently get asked, "How can I develop my strengths?"

I respond, "Pretend that you have them. Act 'as if' you are kind, or forgiving, or curious."

"But how do I do that if I don't know how?"

"Improvisational theater would tell you to make it up. You have probably observed someone acting in that way in your lifetime. Take that next meeting of yours and try acting 'as if' you have that strength."

One way to act "as if" is to read a piece of literature or a speech that embodies that strength. In this book, the discussion of each character strength is augmented with at least one monologue, poem, or famous speech to be performed aloud.

Don't just read them silently to yourself. Reading silently means you are only taking in the text with your eyes. In addition to helping you act "as if," reading aloud:

- Sharpens your focus
- Connects you to your emotions and imagination
- Increases your vocabulary
- Results in greater comprehension
- Gives you an opportunity to play
- Exercises your body
- Challenges your use of intonation
- Improves listening and reading skills

These benefits are worth the discomfort of going outside your comfort zone and the fear of looking foolish.

Reading aloud helps you explore your ZPD and expand yourself. Literally, by taking on new characters out loud, you can build character strengths.

So try it right now. Put down your coffee. Stop checking your email. **Read the following aloud,** and start to embody the strengths of zest, bravery, and appreciation of beauty and excellence.

Chesapeake **(Monologue)**

by Lee Blessing

(This character is a senator addressing Congress to urge for Arts funding.)

Are there miracles in life? I for one know that there are. And because I know this, I recognize that there are dimensions of life that we do not understand, that we must explore. If we refuse to do this, if we fail to examine publicly and persistently and collectively the innermost nature of life, we lose the right to call ourselves a society at all. We become merely an aggregation of purposeless spirits, ghosts encased in flesh.

Nearly two hundred years ago we sent Lewis and Clark to go where we could not. To explore a land we knew was ours, but which only they could reach. They brought it back to us. I submit that a similar land, but far vaster, occupies the human soul. Only a few people can find the way there. If we help them go we help ourselves, because they can--they will--bring it back to us. Their discoveries won't all be happy or beautiful. Some will be dangerous. But each will enlarge us. Deepen us. Revive us.

Part 1:

Exploring the 24 VIA Character Strengths

Part 1 explores each character strength in a separate chapter. Each chapter starts with a definition of the character strength quoted or paraphrased from the book, *Character Strengths and Virtues* (CSV) by Christopher Peterson and Martin Seligman. In case you wish to find them in CSV, each definition includes one or more page numbers marked thus: CSV-xxx.

The articles that come next in each chapter contain stories about the ways that character strengths show up in particular settings. These are adaptations of articles that appeared on Positive Psychology News (PPND) between January 2007 and May 2015. Each author has generously granted permission to use his or her article in this book in honor of Christopher Peterson.

Illustrating the articles are original drawings by the artist Kevin Gillespie, who has donated his time and talent to the art in this book.

The editorial goal of Positive Psychology News is to help the general public gain a clear understanding of research findings that contribute to human well-being. Articles tend to connect stories to recent research findings. The versions of the articles included in this book have most of the research citations removed for ease of reading. To find links to the original articles that contain the research citations, curious readers can go to

http://bit.ly/PPNDCharStrengths

To find all the research citations, organized by the various character strengths followed by the applications in the order they appear in the book curious readers can go to:

http://positivepsychologynews.com/books/csm-references

After the article, each chapter includes five actions to build that character strength. We have selected them with permission from a much longer list of actions created by Tayyab Rashid. In addition to containing nearly 3 times as many actions as we have included here, his online resource, *Building Your Strengths,* defines what too much or too little of each strength looks like. He also provides a list of movies that embody character strengths. Tayyab's full list can be found at

http://bit.ly/BuildVIAStrengths

For those that enjoy watching movies that bring character strengths to life, we also suggest the book by Ryan Niemiec and Daniel Wedding, *Positive Psychology at the Movies: Using Films to Build Character Strengths and Well-Being.*

Finally each chapter contains at least one passage to read aloud to bring the character strength to life in your mind and body. Some of these are poems, some are excerpts from speeches or letters, and others are monologues from plays. To understand why we urge you to read these passages aloud, review *Acting 'As If'* page 8.

Appreciation

"Appreciation of beauty and excellence (or simply appreciation) refers to the ability to find, recognize, and take pleasure in the existence of goodness in the physical and social worlds. A person high in this strength frequently feels awe and related emotions (including admiration, wonder, and elevation). A person low on this strength goes about daily life as if wearing blinders to that which is beautiful and moving..." CSV-538

Fringe Benefits of Appreciation

by Sherri Fisher

Today, as I do on most mornings, I pop my ear buds in and take a brisk walk along a route in my neighborhood. I'm moving to the beat of an excellent playlist of my own choosing. The stiff damp wind is out of the east. Though I live more than fifteen miles from the nearest beach, from the scent of the blowing mist I can imagine that the surf is crashing in just a few blocks away. It is still early, and the lead-gray sky is made darker in the places where the fog is still thick. By most people's standards it is not a beautiful day.

None of the other walkers, runners, or bike riders greets me with, "Gorgeous day, isn't it?" Even the usually perky puggle dog on my block sits quietly on his front steps among the first colored leaves that have fallen from a hundred year-old maple tree. Its ancient roots push up through the stone fence at the edge of the property. Just the same, I feel pleasantly filled up by the beautiful things I see, hear, smell, and feel around me.

It may be possible to take this same walk every day and not experience anything new and uplifting. But because I have the strength of appreciation of beauty and excellence, I cannot help but notice everything from the bees buzzing in to find their place in the huge flowers of the butterfly bush to the smell of fall on the breeze to the easiness of the stride of the runner who has just passed me. In the now overgrown front garden of the next house along my walk is a tall stalk with several green milkweed pods not yet ready to pop open. Food for next year's gorgeous Monarch butterflies, I imagine.

Continuing along my usual route I come to the bank parking lot where the damp wind is blowing the scent of "eau de dumpster" my way. I pick my pace up to a jog. Another quarter of a mile down the road an antique house has the windows boarded up. A developer has uprooted all of the trees and scraped off the grass and topsoil from the property. Not long ago two families lived here with their small children and dogs. I watched them water the potted plants on stone front steps that are now missing.

"Who let them do this?" I ask myself with my beauty and excellence voice.

As with all strengths, appreciation of beauty and excellence feels natural and right to the person who has it. I know that I have this strength because things that are not either beautiful or excellent (admittedly to me) push this strengths button. I remember to say to myself, "I'm having a B and E moment" when I start to feel the "ick" of disgust (the opposite of elevation) rising within me. I even have a friend who shares the strength with me, and we regularly text each other with pictures or commentary about our moments.

As a strength, appreciation of beauty and excellence is more than just our preferences in dumpster location or local property development. Awe, wonder, and elevation are elicited by the perception and contemplation of beauty and excellence.

Imagine an awe-inspiring double rainbow against an angry grey sky. Any uplifting sensory experience can lead to these transcendent emotions.

An additional way to consider appreciation of beauty and excellence is to think of the pleasurable openness and awe we feel when enjoying the highly developed skills and virtues of others. This awe may be experienced in the incredible "Wow!" of watching a basketball free-throw shot go through the net without even touching the rim or the seemingly impossible leap of the soccer goalkeeper making a save.

Figure 1: Admire expertise

It could be the almost dumbstruck quality we feel after watching a film that has elicited such intense emotion that we have nothing to say about it at first.

It could be the wonder we feel when reading an author's clarity of thought presented in a few artfully chosen words.

It could be the deep admiration we feel when hearing someone thank the firefighter who rescued people and pets from a burning building.

Unlike a more cognitive strength like curiosity, appreciation of beauty and excellence has a strong set of emotions connected to it. You know that you have this strength because you feel it strongly, not just because you think, "Isn't that lovely? I wonder who created it."

There are bodily responses and facial expressions that go with this strength, such as wide-open eyes, an open mouth, goose bumps, tears, and a lump in the throat that typically accompany experiences that stimulate amazed admiration.

In addition to things like music, art, architecture, sport, and nature, religious and spiritual experiences are often connected to appreciation of beauty and excellence. This strength is a pathway for moral and spiritual advancement. A sense of the power of the divine is intimately connected with awe. Profound gratitude for both the beauties of creation and the powers of the natural world are evidence of this strength.

Some people might be scared by a thunderstorm while others might be awed. In those moments, the person with the strength of appreciation of beauty and excellence is able to transcend ego and instead be moved to an awareness of the vastness and amazement that the world has to offer. Time slows down. In such moments a person may feel drawn to future opportunities for using the strength.

To feel expansive, positive, and grateful, develop the strength of appreciation of beauty and excellence. You will become an inspiration to the people around you.

<u>Five Actions to Build Appreciation</u>

by Tayyab Rashid

1. Notice at least one instance of natural beauty around you every day (sunrise, sunset, clouds, sunshine, snowfall, rainbows, trees, moving leaves, birds chirping, flowers, fruits and vegetables, etc.). Bring back the mental picture when your surroundings feel unpleasant.

2. Note weekly how the goodness of other people affects your life. Appreciate the beauty of positive human behavior.

3. For your next three projects, pick at least one to do particularly mindfully. Instead of doing it meticulously, prioritize to do it with care and an appreciation for beauty.

4. Notice how others appreciate beauty and excellence through specific words, expressions, gestures, and actions. See if you notice them admiring aspects of life that you aren't typically aware of.

5. Notice and admire excellence of someone's character strengths. Appreciate them as a whole person with unique aspects.

All the Way Home (Monologue)

by Tad Mosel

Read aloud to explore the strength of appreciation of beauty and excellence.

Andrew: I tell you, Rufus, if anything ever makes me believe in God, or Life After Death, it'll be what happened this afternoon in Greenwood Cemetery. There were a lot of clouds, but they were blowing fast, so there was lots of sunshine too. Right when they began to lower your father into the ground, into his grave, a cloud came over and there was a shadow just like iron, and a perfectly magnificent butterfly settled on the coffin, just rested there, right over the breast, and stayed there, just barely making his wings breathe like a heart. He stayed there all the way down, Rufus, until it grated against the bottom like a – rowboat. And just when it did, the sun came out just dazzling bright and he flew up and out of that – hole in the ground, straight up into the sky, so high I couldn't even see him anymore. Don't you think that's wonderful, Rufus? If there are any such things as miracles, then *that's* surely miraculous.

Bravery

"Bravery is the ability to do what needs to be done, despite fear." Bravery may mean physical bravery, acting in spite of fear of bodily injury or death. It may mean moral bravery, doing what one knows is right in spite of fear of ridicule or exclusion. It may also mean psychological bravery, facing anxieties in spite of fear of loss of stability. CSV-199, CSV-214

What is a Unit of Courage?

by Lisa Sansom

I interviewed Robert Biswas-Diener, author of the book, *The Courage Quotient*. We explored courage, strengths, self-doubt, and the future of positive psychology.

Lisa: To prepare for our interview, I asked my children for their questions about courage. My 10-year-old wanted to know, "How do you measure courage? What would be a unit of courage?"

Robert: That's an awesome question. Kids always ask the best questions. I'd say we could call it a *will power* like a *candle power* is a unit of light. A will power would be a unit of courage, because in large part, courage is the will to action despite fear. The strengths constellation of self-regulation and willpower is really the crux of courage.

Lisa: What is your definition of courage?

Robert: When I was looking at the work that others have done on courage, I realized that there were certain hallmark features: there has to be perceived personal risk, the presence of fear, and an uncertain outcome. Those are the three critical components. Brave actions take place despite the fear, the risk, and the uncertainty.

Lisa: Your initial examples of courage are what people might expect, typical stories about physical courage. What was the most unusual example you came across in writing your book?

Robert: We do think first about the most physical acts of courage. They seem to be the easiest to understand. Yet one executive said that the most courageous thing he does is to hire people. When you hire people, you invest money in them. You change your team dynamics. You change your culture. Firing someone is more straightforward, and the outcome is much more known. You might worry in the very short-term about an emotional backlash, but that's pretty tame because six months down the road, there isn't much consequence. When you hire someone, there could be enormous consequences six months down the road.

Another example that I came up with was the idea of beginning new things: going to school, getting a new job, marrying someone, moving to a new city. These are very everyday occurrences, but they are acts of optimism and bravery.

Lisa: Are there ranges also within the day-to-day?

Robert: This starts to get to one of my favorite topics about courage, which is the notion of courage blindness. We tend to write off our own history of bravery by saying, "Oh I just did what anyone would have done," or "If I were really brave, I would have..." But these comparisons belittle valid acts of bravery.

Lisa: What benefit would people get from honoring their own courageous stories?

Robert: Essentially, the same benefits that they would derive from understanding their strengths in general: self-regard, self-esteem, more energy, and perseverance towards difficult tasks. This helps people see themselves in their own best light.

Lisa: What would you say is really important about courage?

Robert: When I inscribe the book for people, I've been writing, "Courage is the shortest route to the good life." I think courage is synonymous with the good life. Fears are all very normal and rational, but fear holds us back from actions that would make life rich and rewarding. People who live a fully engaged life are exhibiting some measure of courage. Courage indicates a willingness to try.

However fear is also a gift, and self-doubt is a gift with enormous signaling value. Sometimes we are doubtful because it's healthy to question ourselves. That sort of reflection is important in coaching and a great process to engage in. But you don't want that fear to hold you back, unless it should. There is definitely a balancing act. Courage is also wisdom: knowing when to act and when not to act.

Figure 2: Be brave in the face of danger

Lisa: Some people say that courage only emerges when you need it. Is it an actual character trait that exemplifies people over time?
Robert: This echoes my general thinking about character traits. I think of them as potentials. They are dormant, but not equally dormant in each person. Someone who is creative is more prone to creativity. The person who is courageous is more prone to

courage. It doesn't mean that you will be courageous in every situation all of the time. Even a minor situational change, like a few more seconds to think and act, could make a big difference.

Lisa: Would you encourage people to increase their courage?

Robert: I do. If you recognize that your willingness to act has to outweigh your fear, and that life is a series of actions, then yes, people should increase their courage quotients. Unless you think you're already optimally courageous, but most of us are not optimally courageous across all domains all of the time. Some people are over-confident, or too courageous.

Lisa: What is the most misunderstood aspect of courage?

Robert: It's a common misconception that courage is only physical. Also, people believe that courage is a trait and can't be learned. People also wrongly believe that courage is something that other people have, and they don't. I defy you to show me someone who hasn't shown courage at some point.

Lisa: You gave a courage prize based on invited nominations. Were most nominations for physical courage?

Robert: No, they weren't. This is a sticky question that I haven't been able to resolve. There is an American notion that facing a chronic illness is courageous. Yet a European told me that was crazy: there is no act of heroism in facing illness. What else could you do? That's not a politically correct thing to say around here, but there may be something to it. If we say that people facing chronic illness are brave, we need to substantiate it. Most of the nominees for the courage prize were people facing chronic pain or illness. Yet is it fair to saddle the mantle of courage on these patients? It might make for interesting research. If you present a fictitious cancer patient to people, but manipulate the data to change her age, for example, would that change how courageous they thought she was? Having cancer does not automatically qualify you as being brave.

I also make the argument in the book that kids aren't brave, and people freak out about that. But Chris Peterson did studies asking parents what character strengths they think their children have, and only a few selected bravery. Kids are generally fearful. When I wrote this, I thought that it was pretty uncontroversial. Courage is about self-regulation, and so children won't be as self-regulated as adults – duh! But it hit such a button in people.

Lisa: But if we say children are more fearful, are they being courageous by children standards, where it might not be courageous by adult standards?

Robert: Well sure, but kids are generally held back by fears: new foods, going into the basement, jumping into the pool. Of course kids can be brave, but it's not a defining characteristic.

Lisa: Would you ever want to see a journal dedicated to courage?

Robert: I've never been asked that before. What a great question. Do I think that courage is a broad enough umbrella that it would merit continued research and assessment? Yes, I do. It's interesting how little research there is on courage. There is lots of research on happiness. It's a concern that touches us all, of course. I think that courage is every bit as important as happiness. Without courage, you can't have a good or full life. Courage is a topic that deserves not just my book, but twenty best-selling books.

Five Actions to Build Bravery

by Tayyab Rashid

1. Speak up for or write about an unpopular idea in a group. Be respectful of other opinions without backing down from yours.
2. Ask difficult questions that help you and others face reality. Be gentle and kind, but don't keep questions inside merely because they are hard to express or answer.
3. Clarify your values by thinking about how best they have served you in challenging situations. Also consider ways in which your values have hindered you, and ways to change this in the future.
4. Identify an area in which you generally shy away from confrontations. Practice the phrases, the tones, and the mannerisms that will enable you to effectively confront the situation next time.
5. Collect contemporary stories of bravery in everyday life situations. Save newspaper or magazine clippings about courageous acts.

Victory Speech (Excerpt)

By Winston Churchill

May 10, 1940

Read aloud to explore the strength of bravery.

We have before us an ordeal of the most grievous kind, and many, many months of struggle and suffering.

You ask, what is our policy?

I say it is to wage war by land, sea, and air. War with all our might and with all the strength God had given us, and to wage war against a monstrous tyranny never surpassed in the dark and lamentable catalogue of human crime. That is our policy.

You ask what is our aim?

I can answer in one word. It is victory. Victory at all costs – victory in spite of terrors – Victory, however long and hard the road may be.

So I say to the House that I have nothing to offer but blood, toil, tears, and sweat [...]

But I take up my task with buoyancy and hope. I feel sure that our cause will not be suffered to fail among men. At this time I feel entitled to claim the aid of all, and I say, "Come then, let us go forward together with our united strength."

Creativity

Creativity involves producing original ideas and behaviors that are adaptive, making a positive contribution to self and/or others. All humans have creativity to some degree, creating novel sentences that have never been spoken before. People high in the character strength of creativity are able to generate original solutions that have an adaptive impact beyond their immediate circles. CSV-110

Be Creative Like a Child

by Tom Heffner

"Son, what is that in your underwear?" I asked, puzzled by the white patch flashing from the middle of his underclothing. We had just finished dinner, and as part of our nightly routine, I was drawing his bath when I spotted something out of place. It turns out my then three-year-old son had swiped one of his mother's menstrual pads in the morning and using the adhesive patches, affixed it to his underwear.

"Look Papa, if I have an accident, my underwear won't get dirty. That's a good idea, right, Papa!"

I had to admit he was right. Moreover, it was a creative solution to his ongoing challenge of potty training. I could not help but chuckle and admire his ingenuity. Since that experience, my son has continued to display imaginative behaviors, learning to express his signature strength of creativity, as well as to identify his other signature strengths.

Creativity, as a character strength is quite straightforward. It is the ability to generate novel and adaptive ideas that positively affect our lives or the lives of the people around us.

The ability to be creative gives us the confidence to meet any problem, challenge, or opportunity that comes our way. Life, both

28

personal and professional, is full of challenges, problems, and opportunities.

Having creative confidence to meet life's challenges and problems helps us avoid feeling helpless. Avoiding perceived helplessness is an important way to maintain well-being.

Figure 3: Try out new ideas

If we believe the logic and science behind these arguments, then the next reasonable question is how do we become more creative? The answer is simple but at the same time not easy: think and act like kids! Children are the most creative and curious group of people you will ever meet. They come into this world driven by curiosity so that they can make sense of the world around them. Their curiosity constantly encourages them to seek out new, varied, and exploratory actions and ideas. By extension, that curiosity drives their creativity and imagination.

Children are willing to think very differently and to try things that seem wrong, embarrassing, contradictory, and even nonsensical. They are not afraid to be wrong and do not accept limitations or constraints.

A good example of this creativity in action was when my then five year-old son and I were building a model rocket. After we had finished building the rocket but before we packed the parachute, my son asked if we could attach a toy army man to the parachute.

"No, we can't do that, son," I replied to him.

"Why not, it will be cool to watch him float down," he responded.

As an electrical engineer, I patronizingly told him, "No son, it will throw the balance off and the parachute will tangle, it won't work." But, as kids do, he persisted until I relented. Later that day, we launched the rocket with the toy army man aboard, and lo and behold, his idea to create a manned model rocket was successful.

As someone who works as an engineer and innovation consultant within my organization, I see the value of that kind of creativity every day. But I can also tell you that it's not easy to think and act with a child-like curiosity and creativity. Nonetheless, what follows here are a few ways to regain your creative confidence. With practice and commitment, you can rediscover that childlike creativity we all have within us.

This is going to seem painfully obvious, but if you want to do things differently or create new and different ideas, then you need to talk to people who are not just like you. For example, let's say you are an investment banker looking to create new investment strategies for your portfolio. If all you do is work with other investment bankers, what are the odds you will create a truly new and different strategy? Probably very low.

But what if you looked beyond your initial circle of colleagues? What if you started asking teachers how they invest their time and resources to produce a high performing student? Or what if you spoke with military leaders in order to see how they invest their resources, their human capital, and their time in young officers to produce future leaders? Now, if we ask that same question, what are the odds you will create a truly new investment strategy for your bank? Probably much higher.

Different perspectives and different experiences can yield very different ideas. Make it a priority to meet someone different from you.

Stop thinking of your ideas as fully baked. Every idea can be thought of as a hypothesis. Just as we learned in grade school, we should always test our hypothesis with an experiment. Each time we conduct an experiment, we put forth a new prototype or idea to test. I do this all the time as an engineer when I'm designing a new hardware device, such as a new antenna. I always learn something new by observing what worked, what failed, and what surprised me. But you don't have to be an engineer to prototype your ideas.

Let's take a look at our political elections, for example. Politicians use the primaries as their experiments all the time. They prototype new political ideas at events, such as town hall meetings, debates, and TV appearances, so that they can gather feedback from voters on what works and doesn't work.

The key takeaway for you is to test out your ideas on other people, gather feedback, and iterate them by building on the feedback and/or ideas of others.

One of my favorite approaches to being creative is to use *design thinking*. This is a human centered design approach that emphasizes the generation of lots of ideas, rapid prototyping, and diverse perspectives.

One of the ways we generate lots of ideas is to brainstorm using the following rules from OpenIDEO.

http://bit.ly/BrainstormRules

- **Defer Judgment**: The best way to let ideas flow is to table our critiques to encourage positive emotions in our participants. When we experience more positive emotions we actually become more creative.

- **Encourage wild ideas**: Wild ideas serve two purposes. They push us out of our comfort zone into new and different areas, and they also create a fun environment where we are more likely to experience positive emotions.

- **Build on the ideas of others**: Some of history's most creative and innovative people built on the ideas of others. Microsoft's first Windows interface was influenced by the first Apple interface. Good ideas are always around us, so look to build on those ideas and make them better.

- **Stay focused on the topic**: Don't lose focus.

- **One conversation at a time**: When people speak over each other you can't hear what they are saying. If you can't hear what they are saying, then chances are your creative ideas are not being heard either.

- **Be visual**: A picture is worth a thousand words. You don't have to be an artist to make your point; a simple stick figure picture can make all the difference in the world when trying to communicate your idea(s).

- **Go for quantity**: To come up with one really outside the box, creative idea, you need a lot of ideas. In my experience, with 4-6 people, you can generate more than 100 ideas within 30-45 minutes of brainstorming.

After you have a long list of ideas, then use judgment to figure out which idea or ideas to prototype first.

Five Actions to Build Creativity

by Tayyab Rashid

1. Create and refine at least one original idea weekly in an area of your interest. To get ideas, peruse existing material on the subject, and think of topics that haven't been addressed.

2. Offer at least one creative solution to challenges of a sibling or a friend. Practice being open to their creative ideas as well as your own. Brainstorm ideas on a challenging task with your friends. Observe the ways that they think creatively.

3. Read about famous creative people and identify what made them unique. Think about the unique aspects of your own life and how you could channel them for creative purposes.

4. Use leftovers (food, stationery and such) to make new products. Consider the artistic or practical uses for items before you throw them away.

5. Look for different and creative ways to spend more time at tasks you do best. Try to incorporate them into your work or chores to make these times more enjoyable.

The Real Thing: A Play (Monologue)

by Tom Stoppard

Read these two pieces aloud to explore the strength of creativity.

HENRY: Leave me out of it. They don't count. Maybe Brodie got a raw deal, maybe he didn't. I don't know. It doesn't count. He's a lout with language. I can't help somebody who thinks, or thinks he thinks, that editing a newspaper is censorship, or that throwing bricks is a demonstration while building tower blocks is social violence, or that unpalatable statement is provocation while disrupting the speaker is the exercise of free speech...Words don't deserve that kind of malarkey. They're innocent, neutral, precise, standing for this, describing that, meaning the other, so if you look after them you can build bridges across incomprehension and chaos. But when they get their corners knocked off, they're no good anymore, and Brodie knocks their corners off. I don't think writers are sacred, but words are. They deserve respect. If you get the right ones in the right order, you can nudge the world a little or make a poem, which children will speak for you when you're dead.

How to Build Creative Confidence (Excerpt)

by David Kelley

So I thought one of the things I'd do today is take you through and show you what this journey looks like. To me, that journey looks like Doug Dietz. Doug Dietz is a technical person. He designs medical imaging equipment, large medical imaging equipment. He's worked for GE, and he's had a fantastic career. But at one point he had a moment of crisis.

He was in the hospital looking at one of his MRI machines in use when he saw a young family. There was a little girl, and that little girl was crying and was terrified. And Doug was really disappointed to learn that nearly 80 percent of the pediatric patients in this hospital had to be sedated in order to deal with his MRI machine. And this was really disappointing to Doug, because before this time he was proud of what he did. He was saving lives with this machine. But it really hurt him to see the fear that this machine caused in kids.

About that time he was [...] at Stanford taking classes. He was learning about our process about design thinking, about empathy, about iterative prototyping. And he would take this new knowledge and do something quite extraordinary. He would redesign the entire experience of being scanned. And this is what he came up with.

He turned it into an adventure for the kids. He had the walls painted to establish a horizon line, and then he had vinyl graphics applied to walls, floor, scanner, and even the technologist's window to set the scene of a pirate ship. He got the operators retrained by people who know kids, like children's museum people. And now when the kid comes, it's an experience. They talk to them about the noise and the movement of the ship. And when they come, they say, "Okay, you're going to go into the pirate ship, but be very still because we don't want the pirates to find you."

And the results were super dramatic. So from something like 80 percent of the kids needing to be sedated, to something like 10 percent of the kids needing to be sedated. And the hospital and GE were happy too. Because you didn't have to call the anesthesiologist all the time, they could put more kids through the machine in a day. So the quantitative results were great. But Doug's results that he cared about were much more qualitative. He was with one of the mothers waiting for her child to come out of the scan. And when the little girl came out of her scan, she ran up to her mother and said, "Mommy, can we come back tomorrow?" (Laughter)

And so I've heard Doug tell the story many times, of his personal transformation and the breakthrough design that happened from it, but I've never really seen him tell the story of the little girl without a tear in his eye.

To see Doug Dietz discuss transforming medical machines with children in mind, go to
http://bit.ly/DougDietzTEDx

Curiosity

"Curiosity, interest, novelty-seeking, and openness to experience represent one's intrinsic desire for experience and knowledge. Curiosity involves the active recognition, pursuit, and regulation of one's experiences in response to challenging opportunities." CSV, p. 125

"Curious people pursue experiential novelty, variety, and challenge." CSV-98

Curiosity as the Engine of Well-being

by Kathryn Britton

I interviewed Todd Kashdan, a professor of psychology at George Mason University and author of the book, *Curious? Discover the Missing Ingredient to a Fulfilling Life.* Here are some of the questions we discussed together.

Kathryn: What prompted you to write your book on curiosity?

Todd Kashdan: I wanted to write about curiosity because it has been neglected, even though there are few things in our arsenal that are so consistently and highly related to every facet of well-being including our needs for belonging, for meaning, for confidence, for autonomy, for spirituality, for achievement, for creativity. The only books out there are getting dusty on academic library shelves. Scientists should write books themselves to get the science out to people.

Kathryn: What inspiration kept you going while you were writing it?

Todd: I have always been an anxiety researcher, especially social anxiety that shows up in people that have profound levels of shyness and fear about being evaluated. Then I started seeing people who had energizing and profoundly meaningful social interactions. I started asking them about their motivations and feelings in the midst of social interaction. What kept arising was

37

"I felt interested," or "I was curious." I realized that curiosity is the counter-motivation to anxiety.

When people are dealing with new people, and new challenges, they're faced with a conflict, "Do I escape the situation so I can't fail and look like a fool? Or do I approach and act on my curiosity, and potentially expand my skills, learn more about my strengths, and find out what rewards are available?" I realized that this conflict between anxiety and curiosity is a fundamental part of everyday lives. Then I realized I would have to study curiosity if I really wanted to understand anxiety.

Curiosity and anxiety work in tandem. It's not the case that when you're curious there's no anxiety, or when you're anxious there's no curiosity. They work in all sorts of different combinations.

Kathryn: How has it affected you to shift from studying anxiety alone to studying anxiety coupled with curiosity?

Todd: It has made me realize that the fundamental objective of my life is not to be happy or have a high frequency of positive emotions, but to have a rich, meaningful existence. That's what I want to inspire in other people as well. In such an existence, people are going to have an abundance of both positive and negative experiences. If you don't make mistakes and have negative emotions and moments of intense anxiety, it means you're not taking risks. When you live trying to avoid threats, you can't possibly be creative, and you can't discover your strengths and figure out how to use them in your life.

So, for me it's a shift from looking for the positive to looking to live a life that matters. It's about experimenting, exploring, and discovering. The cool thing about writing this book and doing ten years of research on curiosity is that I am very aware of deciding between the familiar and the new. I can pick my favorite entrée at a restaurant, or I can go with the chef's specialty, which is exotic and interesting, but I may hate. I find *high risk, high reward* is a nice way to live life.

Kathryn: So you're suggesting a shift away from "Let's be positive," to "Let's accept anxiety as a necessary part of a life that involves taking risks."

Todd: Yes, and sometimes we feel anxious because something matters to us. This book argues that we should be doing things that are aligned with what we're most passionate about. Following curiosity helps us explore and identify the things that are important to us.

Curiosity is important for other aspects of well-being. Think about gratitude. It is one of the most profound predictors of having happiness in life. But how can I be grateful without asking, "Who in my social environment is giving me help that I may not be acknowledging?" So curiosity is the engine that allows me to be grateful.

What about finding strengths and using them in new ways? That implies questions like "What am I about? When am I at my best? When am I at my most energized?" Self-exploration is about being curious. It's curiosity directed inward.

Kathryn: So would you say that curiosity is one of the driving engines of well-being?

Todd: In my book, I call curiosity the engine of growth. You can't find your passions or purpose in life without trial and error experimentation. Curiosity is a mechanism that helps you create and discover meaning in your life. In the process you catch glimpses of happiness as it ebbs and flows in your lifetime.

I worry about the literal obsession with happiness being the fundamental objective of life. A fulfilling life is about a matrix of elements. What ingredients are related to the most elements? What ingredients are related to the elements that I'm trying to change in my life, or in my client's life, or in this organization? Can we give names to the ingredients so that people can talk with great precision about things that lead to positive outcomes?

When we focus just on happiness, it's so broad and nebulous that we can't get our hands around it. We need to be more specific about the elements that are already there and the ones we haven't built into life yet. Some people have an energizing, enthusiastic work climate, but they're ignoring spirituality or other people's needs for love or profound sources of meaning in life. If we focus on these other elements, would we get even more than an energetic, highly enthusiastic workplace? I don't know. These are questions that we haven't explored yet.

How well does someone deal with stressful emotions? How about achievement and creativity? These are all dimensions of well-being. If every person has a profile, then we can explore his or her well-being in greater precision. Someone might say, "Now that you mention it, those are areas I haven't thought about much that might be important for me to work on." But when we focus at a broad level on happiness or having a fulfilling life, we potentially miss the picture that each person has his or her own individualized profile for how life is going.

Kathryn: I can hear a lot of curiosity when you talk about individuals and how they differ.

Todd: Yes, and exploration and experimenting is part of everything that we do to increase well-being. What I wanted to do with this book was to take this seemingly simple emotional experience and give it back to people so that they can use it intentionally instead of passively letting curiosity arise when novel, captivating things happen. Curiosity is a strength that people can wield. I can decide to seek new things. I can decide to look at a person from new perspectives. I can ask people what they were like before I met them. I can ask my romantic partner what she does when I'm not there. Looking at what it means to respond well when things go right, it's all about being intrigued by good things that happen to the people around you.

Kathryn: Do you think that there's a great deal of variability in curiosity from person to person?

Todd: Absolutely. We all have different genetic predispositions that affect how sensitive we are to novelty and whether we get upset in unfamiliar and uncertain situations. There is also a major age effect. Children have boundless curiosity to explore.

Figure 4: Experience wonder

Then there's something that occurs when we enter adulthood. We learn the rules, we want to develop some closure, we want to feel intelligent, and we want to feel some level of certainty and structure in our lives. When we learn what the rules are at the workplace, which are different from those in a funeral parlor, which are different from those in an elevator, which are different from those at a cocktail party, what falls to the wayside is the lust for new things. We get caught up in the struggle to control uncertainty, which we can't actually do.

Kathryn: What was the most surprising thing that you came across when you were working on the book?

Todd: I think the brain science research on Parkinson's and Alzheimer's disease. One of the first markers of Parkinson's and Alzheimer's at the neurological level is inability to manage and deal with novelty, an early sign of degeneration. It includes not only an unwillingness to go seek out the unfamiliar and a clinging to the familiar, but an actual aversion to being faced with something never seen before. Dopamine is linked up with anticipating rewards, and so it's closely linked to curiosity. Dopamine kicks in when we see that there's something novel. Dopamine circuits are short-circuited in the early stages of Parkinson's and Alzheimer's disease.

Doing actively novel activities buffers the age-related cognitive decline and reduces the risk for Parkinson's and Alzheimer's. Thus exploring new things appears to be a potential antidote to degenerative brain diseases.

Kathryn: You've explained how curiosity relates to strengths and gratitude. How does it relate to mindfulness?

Todd: I think curiosity is one of the two major dimensions of mindfulness. You can't have mindfulness without being curious. Most people focus on the gentle guiding of attention towards the present moment, focusing on a chosen target of attention, and gently guiding attention from things that distract.

The second part of mindfulness is the quality of attention. I find "non-judgmental" a negative, off-putting term. The quality of attention is about having an open and receptive and curious attitude towards whatever is the target of your attention. I think this gets lost in the definition.

Kathryn: Are there different kinds of curiosity?

Todd: I had a study where we asked over 500 people what are the things that make them most curious. The two most frequent categories were being curious about other people's lives and trying to figure themselves out – introspection. We don't talk enough about the value of introspection, being curious about the self. You can't set goals or spot strengths without introspection. You can't get there without curiosity.

Kathryn: So do you have a research question that you'd really like to see somebody address?

Todd: Yes! There are people that are addressing this question, but I think it hasn't fully been answered yet: How do you maintain passion, commitment, and intimacy in long-term relationships?

My first mentor, Arthur Aron, had a cool finding. First you have romantic couples do novel and exciting things together. Not just something pleasant, it has to be new territory. Then you have them bring up unresolved conflicts. They were much more agreeable, open-minded, and warm toward each other after sharing a novel activity.

That hits the value of being curious, being intrigued with your partner. Lives are getting longer. If you get married or committed in a relationship at age 30, how do you keep a relationship for 70 years? Seven decades. That's the research that I want to see done — really difficult, longitudinal research to get at how people behave in their everyday lives that can maintain that excitement and that intrigue, and thus keep that relationship alive and vital.

What do extremely happy, passionate couples look like? What can we learn from them? Who are the couples that can be our Martin Luther Kings and Mother Teresas of marriage? I want exemplars. I want to be able to whip out examples that show how these couples behave differently. How do they synchronize with each other? How open are they to letting each other evolve separately and together? What space do they provide for each other? These are difficult things to measure, but too important not to study.

Five Actions to Build Curiosity

by Tayyab Rashid

1. Expand your knowledge in an area of interest through books, journals, magazines, TV, radio, or Internet, for half an hour, three times a week. Speak to an expert in this area to get recommendations for good resources.

2. Eat food of a different culture that you have little or no exposure to. Explore the food's cultural context and become aware of your thoughts on it. Share a meal with a friend, and compare your impressions.

3. Connect with a person of a different culture and spend at least an hour, twice a month, learning about his/her culture. Be inquisitive, non-judgmental, and open about your own culture.

4. Visit at least one new town, state, or country yearly. If possible, explore it on foot or by bicycle rather than by car. Try to speak to some of the local people to learn more about their community.

5. Get engaged in more open-ended learning experiences (e.g., making ice cream to understand physics and chemistry or taking a yoga class to understand different muscle groups). Bring a friend and compare thoughts after the experience.

On Teaching

by Kahlil Gibran

Read aloud to explore the strength of curiosity.

No man can reveal to you aught but that which already lies half asleep in the dawning of your knowledge.

The teacher who walks in the shadow of the temple, among his followers, gives not of his wisdom but rather of his faith and his lovingness.

If he is indeed wise he does not bid you enter the house of wisdom, but rather leads you to the threshold of your own mind.

The astronomer may speak to you of his understanding of space, but he cannot give you his understanding.

The musician may sing to you of the rhythm, which is in all space, but he cannot give you the ear that arrests the rhythm nor the voice that echoes it.

And he who is versed in the science of numbers can tell of the regions of weight and measure, but he cannot conduct you thither.

For the vision of one man lends not its wings to another man.

And even as each one of you stands alone in God's knowledge, so must each one of you be alone in his knowledge of God and in his understanding of the earth.

Fairness

People who are strong in Fairness are concerned that all people get their fair shares. They are careful not to use others. They tend to be committed to social justice, treating others with kindness, and making personal judgments about what is right that may not align with what others around them are doing.

"Fairness is the product of moral judgment—the process by which people determine what is morally right, what is morally wrong, and what is morally proscribed." CSV-392

Monkeys and the Goddess on Fairness

by Sean Doyle

When my son was in middle school he argued about everything. Everything. No perceived injustice or imagined grievance, great or small, was off limits.

I understand that adolescence is a self-limiting disorder that we all outgrow. But that offers little solace when trying to navigate life with a middle school son. So I did what any other parent soaked in positive psychology would do: I had him take the Values in Action inventory to identify his strengths of character. (It is at this point in the story that my children call me a nerd.)

Andy's two highest strengths were fairness and bravery. No wonder he seemed to fight about everything.

Fairness is one of the virtues most valued in our culture, the second most prevalent character strength behind only kindness.

It is one of only five strengths said to be a high match with the demands of work. The full list includes fairness, integrity, open-Mindedness, perspective, and zest. We want fair judges and police, fair bosses and parents. When negotiating business deals or legislative policy, pleas to fairness soften the other's demands.

Fairness predicts students' grades as well as their satisfaction in college. In the wild, baboons groom those who are unfairly

46

picked on. In classrooms, students who score higher on civic strengths such as leadership and fairness are more popular, even than their classmates high in love and kindness.

Fairness was so highly valued by the Greeks and Romans that they clothed her in a stola, gave her scales and a cornucopia and made her a goddess. When people became too violent and ruled by self-interest and all the other gods abandoned the earth, Astraea, the Greek's "star maiden" was the last of the immortals to leave. She stayed to plead for fairness among humankind. Fairness is so highly valued by monkeys that they will reject tasty, but inequitable rewards. Some chimpanzees will even refuse to take a preferred food unless the partner also receives it.

Figure 5: Weigh both sides

What is this virtue immortalized as a goddess and valued by apes?

Fairness is related to justice, but it is something different. In the Nichomachean Ethics, Aristotle distinguished between legal justice and conscious justice, that is, between what is lawful and

47

what is fair and right. When we are unable to manage a clash between different rights or values, we have our laws to fall back on. But in a different time or context or place the laws might have been different. What is considered just might have been different. Æquitas (equity) on the other hand, the Roman Goddess with her scales, is what allows the law to be changed when there are circumstances that mere mortal lawmakers could not foresee. Fairness assumes symmetry and evenness.

Even then, we struggle with what is fair. Both liberals and conservatives root fairness in reciprocity, yet it is expressed differently. Fairness means equality to people on the left of the political spectrum, where it means proportionality to people on the right. Contrast the view that the wealthy exploit those on the bottom of the socio-economic ladder with the view that people should be rewarded based on what they contribute, even if that means they receive something very different than others do.

Courageous and driven by fairness, my 13-year-old son fought against perceived injustice even if doing so was contrary to his own interests. Framed this way, what once seemed just querulous behavior took on a new quality. Gandhi, Mandela, and Martin Luther King Jr. changed history by combining the same two strengths.

But our strengths can sometimes trip us up. What for one person may be a matter of fundamental fairness, to others may seem pointless or seditious. Our strengths are not weaknesses. They really are strengths. However they can also cast shadows.

If Fairness _is_ the most authentic expression of who you are, then that is also the lens through which you see the world. You expect that others will treat you fairly. You expect strangers to treat one another fairly. But the world in which we live is not always fair. We do not all start at the same line when the race begins. You may get passed over for a promotion. You may be misled by someone you love. Others may take advantage of you.

Approaching the world as fundamentally fair makes us sensitive to when it is not. This is good and powerful and essential for proportionality and equity in our world. It is how laws are made and changed. It is what calls us to protect the vulnerable.

But if we are not attentive to the biases and wishes cast by our strengths, they can also blind us to other values that may be at stake. You might not see that there were other facts holding the scales in balance.

Keeping looking for that balance. Keep fighting for what is right. Continue to pick up the pebbles one by one and place them in the silver trays of Æquitas. Maybe this tray is a little too heavy. Maybe next time we need to place two on the side that has been neglected. By so doing you bring Astraea, the Fairness goddess, back again. You express that immortal quality that holds us all together.

Five Actions that Build Fairness

by Tayyab Rashid

1. The next time you make a mistake, self-monitor to see whether you admit it. Try to be more forthright about your mistakes in the future.

2. Encourage equal participation of everyone involved in a discussion or activity, especially those who feel left out. Foster a reputation as an "includer."

3. Self-monitor to see whether your judgments are affected by your personal likes and dislikes or are based on principles of justice and fairness. Try to minimize the influence of your personal preferences when making future judgments.

4. Serve on a club or organization that offers unprivileged people a level playing field. Encourage your place of employment to provide a level playing field whenever you see the opportunity.

5. Speak up for your group. Be a voice for the rights of others in a manner that respects people from other groups.

On Civil Resistance (Speech)

by Elizabeth McAlister

Read aloud to explore the strength of Fairness.

You can make things legal, but you can never make it right!

Slavery was once legal. The devastation of our earth for profit is all legal. You can make everything legal, but you can never make it right!

If we blow up the world, when we cut down the last tree, it will all be legal. What does this say about us?

The earth is what we all have in common. We cannot damage it without damaging ourselves.

We are losing 10,000 species a year, the greatest setback on earth since the first flickering of life almost 4 billion years ago.

We live by robbing nature but our standard of living demands it. We are unwilling to live within our means; our way of life is predicated on having more than we need. We destroy the land, exhaust its resources, and exploit human labor.

How could we have allowed it to get so bad...so wrong...so sick?

We've got to learn. With every fiber of our beings we must learn to go out there, make a difference and make this world a better place.

Forgiveness

"Those who consistently let bygones be bygones – not because of negative states and traits like fear, shame, guilt, or permissiveness and not because of external incentives (bribes or damages awarded in civil suits) or threats (restraining orders) but from a positive strength of character – display forgiveness and mercy."

Forgiveness is a strength that is invoked when a person is offended or damaged by a relationship partner. People strong in forgiveness believe that it is important to mend relationships with people that damaged or betrayed them. Forgiveness is an internal state where the person lets go of resentment and does not hold grudges. CSV-432, CSV-446

Who is Forgiveness For?

by Prakriti Tandon

Some 21 months ago, my mother was the victim of an armed robbery. Two gunmen posed as university students looking for housing and manipulated their way into the office that my parents have presided over for nearly 4 decades. They pulled out guns and blunt-force objects from beneath their jackets, bound my mother's hands and feet with duct tape, and demanded to know "where the money was."

My parents had for years kept a reserve of cash in the office for contractors who generally lived hand-to-mouth and needed not just advances to start jobs, but immediate cash payments upon completion. My trusting parents used an honor code in their place of work, leaving these funds in each worker's folder for them to access when they came to the office. There had been petty thefts and burglaries over the years, but the system worked better than not, and despite my mother's wariness and occasional protests, my father's compassion for his workers won out, and the system continued.

Alas, a day would come when their trust would be abused in the most grotesque way. As the first armed assailant, the shorter and stockier of the two, ripped more duct tape from the roll to wrap around my mother's head and mouth, she inquired in her mild and steady voice, "Why are you doing this, son? What do you want?" The perpetrator responded to her maternal sobriquet with an epithet. "Shut up bitch!" he shouted, and struck my gentle mother in the face with the long blunt weapon he wielded.

The FBI agent handling the case still smiles when he hears how my mother called the lead perpetrator "son," as only a mild and compassionate mother could. By now, after several phone conversations and face-to-face meetings with my mother, countless hours spent studying the details of the case, and years of face-to-face encounters with unsavory specimens of humanity, he has a finely tuned radar for good and evil. His smile, a delicate fusion of admiration and bewildered awe, conveys his recognition of my mother as the very best of humanity in the face of the very worst.

What does this story teach us? Revisiting this experience tempts me to tears every time, not just because it is my beloved mother I must envision in this distressing scenario, but also because of the utter perversity of one human being responding so violently to the diametrically opposed compassion of another.

For my mother, revisiting this trauma reminds her (in her words) "to hold them in the light." Translation: forgive their transgressions and seek not their demise, but to uplift them. From whence does this transcendence come? How is my mother able not just to allay her anger, but actually to desire the elevation of her aggressors?

My mother came upon one piece of writing in particular in the aftermath of her trauma that she reverted to time and again to help her navigate the path of healing. Let it be known, she should have earned an honorary psychology degree for her unquenchable thirst for all of our reading materials. She drank up every book I brought home, and still desired more. Poring over one of her favorites, Sonja Lyubomirsky's *The How of Happiness*, she came upon an explanation of forgiveness that made sense to her.

How do we learn to forgive? Forgiving is something that people do for themselves, not just for the people that wronged them. I marvel at the counter-intuitive nature of this statement. Don't we generally think of forgiveness as an altruistic act?

Figure 6: Forgive

It was in watching my mother navigate this ordeal that I understood that the true benefit of forgiveness lies in the more selfish act of allowing it into our lives. During these difficult months, my mother faced a potential punishment that was even weightier than any the perpetrators might receive. She risked life imprisonment from her own anger, her own "unforgiveness," as some call the stress reaction that many victims of an interpersonal transgression experience afterwards.

Former President Bill Clinton asked Nelson Mandela how he was able to bring himself to forgive his jailers, and Mandela responded, "When I walked out of the gate I knew that if I continued to hate these people I was still in prison." Forgiveness seems to be a necessity, not a choice, if one is to move forward in life free, weightless, and resilient.

There is a relationship between forgiveness and resilience. So what might we do to bolster that relationship? How might we maximize the utility of forgiveness as a tool to spring back into a flourishing state after an adverse event? I can just imagine the benefits to victims who seek to forgive not just to enhance their own flourishing, but also to embrace the elevation of their own aggressors.

As the trial date approaches and my mother prepares to face her aggressors once more, she is a paragon of forgiveness and the consequent resilience.

Forgiveness or Revenge?

by Louisa Jewell

Last Sunday I attended the Annual Fire Communion Service at my local church. In this ceremony, each congregant burns a piece of paper containing a brief description of something he or she most wishes to leave behind and lights a candle for one new hope for the coming year. I reflected on what I wanted to let go and wrote it down on a tiny piece of flash paper the church provided. I took my place in line as I watched others throw their paper into the fire. When I found myself next in line I slowly placed my paper close to the fire and as I did that, it instantly ignited and disappeared. Just like that, I felt the burden I had been carrying around for years disappear.

Written on my piece of paper was something I had been carrying around for over 12 years. A very close family member had hurt me very badly many years ago. For my own health and happiness, I decided to completely forgive her by finding compassion for her. I understood why she did what she did, and I forgave her not because I felt what she did was right, but to enable me to let it go. Over the years, repeated forgiveness had offered me no relief, and I began to question if forgiveness were the right thing to do in this case. This is when I started to dig deeper into the downside of forgiveness. Is there any time when it does not make sense?

Now I know that the proposition that forgiveness can have negative consequences (gasp!) flies in the face of extensive research showing the positive effects of forgiveness. In fact, the dozens of studies done on forgiveness certainly give the impression that forgiveness is always the right answer for one's well-being. But like any virtue, I believe the best use of it is in moderation. On one end of the scale, not having the ability to show any forgiveness can leave you isolated and cold, and on the other end of the scale, using forgiveness indiscriminately can leave you feeling weak, which can erode self-respect. The best use of forgiveness is to know how and when to use it.

Now I do not espouse violence to resolve any issue, but I was intrigued by the idea that revenge is not a disease that needs to be eradicated, but rather a natural human behavior that has served an evolutionary purpose. Researcher Michael McCullough asks "Why would a species ... engage in costly behavior such as revenge unless it is associated with a benefit in the currency of fitness? ...What could maintain revenge in humans' behavioral repertoire?" He puts forth three reasons:

Deterring harm: If you harm me, a vengeful program in my mind is activated, and I might hurt you back. Knowing this will make it less likely you will harm me again.

Setting the tone for what is acceptable behavior in society: If you harm me and I harm you back, that sends a message to your community or group, "Don't mess with me, because I will harm you back."

Encouraging cooperation in human societies: How did we make civilization happen? If people punish selfish behavior, then you can get people to cooperate for the common good.

This is not revenge for satisfaction, but rather revenge in the form of imposing consequences for violations. For example, the person who rides the subway for free is imposed a fine, or the woman who is being abused by her husband decides to leave the marriage and bars him from the benefits of the relationship by walking away. If we do not impose costs, what will stop the perpetrator from hurting again? So what guidance can we get for whether forgiveness or revenge is the answer?

Research shows that the spouses who were more forgiving towards partners who rarely behaved negatively experienced more marital satisfaction in the first two years of marriage. But the spouses who were forgiving towards partners that frequently behaved negatively experienced sharper declines in marital satisfaction. Whether forgiving yields positive or negative consequences depends on the perpetrator's subsequent behavior.

If the perpetrator's behavior signals that the victim will be safe and valued, forgiving can bolster the forgiver's self-respect. If the perpetrator fails to make amends and continues to behave in an abusive way, forgiving diminishes the forgiver's self-respect. Thus forgiveness is wise only if the relationship is safe and valuable to the victim.

In my opinion, too much forgiveness is the way abusive relationships continue. People forgive even when the abuse continues. I do not believe that retaliation is the answer, but rather people must stand up for themselves and impose reasonable consequences until their perpetrators see the light. Once safety has been restored, then forgiveness can be a powerful tool to let the transgressions from the past go and move on to more positive pursuits. It is important to maintain your self-respect when forgiving and to avoid feeling used.

To understand the conditions under which forgiving restores or further erodes self-respect, one must understand the factors involved in the decision to forgive. Just as revenge can serve a purpose, forgiveness is also important for the evolution and maintenance of social relationships that are important to human survival. If you want to have positive relationships in a group or team, you need to have a mechanism that allows people to erase ill will in order for relationships to evolve. You can't get valuable relationships to stick if you can't let past grievances go.

If we understand what activates revenge or forgiveness, then we can create environments that make it easier to put forgiveness into practice.

There are three things that activate the forgiveness instinct:

Safety: People are naturally inclined to forgive people who they trust will not hurt them again.

Value: When relationships look like they have long-term value and we can see benefit of restoring relationships, then we are more likely to forgive.

Compassion or Care: We tend to more easily forgive those we have compassion for, often people who unintentionally hurt us.

If we can create this kind of environment at home, at work and in our communities, we will see forgiveness flourish.

Forgiveness had always worked well for me with this one exception. In this case, I had forgiven someone over and over who continued to hurt me intentionally without ever making amends. This had negative effects on my self-respect. When I finally decided that I would no longer accept such behavior in my life, I removed myself from the situation so that I could no longer be hurt. Forgiveness finally felt peaceful, but only after I stood up for myself and regained my self-respect.

Five Actions to Build Forgiveness

by Tayyab Rashid

1. Remember times when you offended someone and were forgiven, then extend this gift to others. Don't demand a formal apology.

2. Understand from the offender's perspective why he/she offended you. Then assess whether your reaction is hurting you more than the offender.

3. Meet a person who offended you in the past, especially if he/she is a family member. Tell them that you have forgiven them, or just be kind in your interaction with them.

4. Pray for the noble behavior of your offender. Think of ways that this person has acted nobly in the past.

5. Identify how a grudge tortures you emotionally. Does it produce disruptive emotions (anger, hatred, fear, worry, sadness, anxiety, jealousy and such)? Write three ways these disruptive emotions affect your behavior.

The Merchant of Venice (Monologue)

by William Shakespeare

Read aloud to explore the strength of forgiveness.

The quality of mercy is not strain'd,
It droppeth as the gentle rain from heaven
Upon the place beneath. It is twice blest:
It blesseth him that gives and him that takes.
'Tis mightiest in the mightiest, it becomes
The throned monarch better than his crown.
His sceptre shows the force of temporal power,
The attribute to awe and majesty,
Wherein doth sit the dread and fear of kings;
But mercy is above this sceptred sway,
It is enthroned in the hearts of kings,
It is an attribute to God himself;
And earthly power doth then show likest God's
When mercy seasons justice. Therefore, Jew,
Though justice be thy plea, consider this,
That, in the course of justice, none of us
Should see salvation. We do pray for mercy,
And that same prayer doth teach us all to render
The deeds of mercy. I have spoke thus much
To mitigate the justice of thy plea,
Which if thou follow, this strict court of Venice
Must needs give sentence 'gainst the merchant there.

Gratitude

"Gratitude is a sense of thankfulness and joy in response to receiving a gift, whether the gift be a tangible benefit from a specific other or a moment of peaceful bliss evoked by natural beauty. Gratitude comes from being aware that one has benefitted from the actions of others." CSV-554

Struggling with Gratitude

by Shannon Polly

One rainy night, I had just come back from taking my youngest daughter to the emergency room. It wasn't a huge deal. Just a raisin up the nose, but apparently the Ear-Nose-and-Throat clinic only services ears. Noses have to go through the ER. Coming home with a healthy kid should have made me feel very grateful. I should have felt grateful that it only took me 2 hours and 15 minutes to discover that there was, in fact, no raisin in her nose any more. I've averaged 4-5 hours every other visit to the ER. I really should have felt grateful that when I left my wallet in the hospital bathroom, someone returned it to security with EVERYTHING in it. The nurse said that in eight years she has never seen a wallet returned before.

I have read the research on gratitude. I've had the honor of teaching gratitude to executives and Army sergeants. Yet I left the ER feeling more annoyed than grateful that my husband urged me to go despite the fact that three months ago a pediatrician visit also found no raisin.

So why is that? Am I just bad at gratitude? Maybe so. It's one of my lower strengths on the Values in Action Character Strength Survey. It's a pretty ironic for a positive psychology practitioner. Or is it just negativity bias? Hedonic adaptation? Or is gratitude just difficult?

I have a coaching client that described seeing the world as a glass half empty. His wife was annoyed by his viewpoint. He asked me if there was something wrong with him. He seemed reassured when I discussed the negativity bias.

We are all hardwired to see the negative first and to weight it more heavily than the positive. That caveman who was appreciating the beauty of the lone flower outside his cave while his relative was scanning the horizon for predatory beasts was probably eaten and didn't pass on his genes. So there are adaptive benefits to scanning for threat. But the problem is that our modern brains equate missing a deadline with threats to life and limb. The same cortisol rushes through our systems, wreaking havoc when it is over expressed.

When good things do happen, we adapt to them. That new car doesn't make us as happy for as long as we thought it would. Humans are very poor at predicting what will make them happy.

Hedonic adaptation can apply to gratitude as well. The most famous positive psychology intervention is the 'Three Good Things" exercise where every night you write down three things that happened to you, what they mean to you, why they happened, and what you can do to get more of each good thing. Research has shown that this exercise leads to better health, better sleep, and better relationships. Yet researchers have also found that when people did it every day, it made them less happy than if they did it once per week. It seems that people adapted to the gratitude exercise.

Don't get me wrong. Gratitude works. I have seen grown men reduced to tears when they started to see the good things in their lives and what they weren't appreciating about their own families. But it isn't easy for everyone. One size does not fit all.

The benefits of gratitude are so far reaching that I know I need to work on this strength. There are a few ways I can do that. First, I try to use my top strengths such as kindness, persistence, and social intelligence, to pull up that bottom strength. For example, I use kindness to help me write thank you notes, but it also takes a bit of persistence when I have many of them to write. My social intelligence helps me to see when someone might not feel like they have been properly thanked, which also helps me to engaged in more gratitude.

Figure 7: Appreciate a gift

Second, I often search for someone who has gratitude as a top strength. Research shows that one way to build your belief in your abilities is to look for role models. In order to build my confidence and competence around gratitude, I try to surround myself with people who are grateful. I had a few pro bono clients when I was going through my coaching certification. One had a top strength of gratitude. He made me feel like a million bucks every time we had a session. He was so grateful for the opportunity to be coached for free, and I worked harder for him. I watched our interactions. How did gratitude become his superpower? I realized part of it was he allowed himself to be helped. He didn't struggle to control everything. As a result he got more done, and made others feel good for helping him.

Third, I remember a particularly unhappy event in my life. Then I ask myself how often I find myself thinking about that event today. Usually the answer is, "Not much." Contrasting it to my current life situation, I realize I am much better off now. The point is not to ignore the past but to develop a new frame of reference in the present from which to view it. Using this new frame, I can see how a stressful event shaped who I am, and I can evaluate what is really important in life.

So what can you do to be more grateful? You can leverage a top strength to pull up a bottom strength. You can seek out a role model who has gratitude as a superpower, and you can contrast a past negative event with your current state. The good news is that if you struggle with gratitude, you can increase it with a little bit of elbow grease.

Five Actions to Build Gratitude

by Tayyab Rashid

1. Every day, select one small yet important thing that you take for granted. Work on being mindful of this thing in the future.

2. Express thanks to all who contributed to your success, no matter how small their contribution might have been. Be aware of the degree to which your success is a product of others' helpful influence in addition to your own hard work.

3. Express thanks without just saying "thanks"– be more descriptive and specific (e.g., "I appreciate your prudent advice"). Observe how people notice detailed gratitude as opposed to a simple, reactionary "Thanks."

4. Set aside at least ten minutes every day to savor a pleasant experience. Decide to withhold any conscious decisions during these ten minutes.

5. Before eating, think of all the people who have contributed to what you are eating. Do this at least once a week.

Farewell to Yankee Fans (Speech)

by Lou Gehrig

Read these two pieces aloud to explore the strength of gratitude.

I have been in ballparks for seventeen years and have never received anything but kindness and encouragement.

Look at these grand men.

Which of you wouldn't consider it the highlight of his career to associate with them for even one day?

When the New York Giants, a team you would give your right arm to beat, sends you a gift, that's something!

When everybody down to the groundkeepers remember you with trophies, that's something.

When you have a father and mother who work all their lives so that you can have an education, that's something.

When you have a wife who has been a tower of strength and shown more courage than you dreamed existed, that's something.

So I close in saying that I might have had a tough break – but today I consider myself the luckiest man on the face of the earth.

Otherwise (Poem)
by Jane Kenyon

I got out of bed
on two strong legs.
It might have been
otherwise. I ate
cereal, sweet
milk, ripe, flawless
peach. It might
have been otherwise.
I took the dog uphill
to the birch wood.
All morning I did
The work I love.

At noon I lay down
with my mate. It might
have been otherwise.
We ate dinner together
at a table with silver
candlesticks. It might
have been otherwise.
I slept in a bed
in a room with paintings
on the walls, and
planned another day
just like this day.
But one day, I know,
It will be otherwise.

Hope

"Hope and optimism represent a stance toward the future and the goodness it might hold." "Thinking about the future, expecting that desired events and outcomes will occur, [...] galvanize goal-directed actions." Even in the face of setbacks, people with this strength look forward to the next opportunity, making plans to do better. CSV-526, CSV-570

Restoring Hope

by Doug Turner

As I meet with individuals and couples, either in my role as a church leader or in my role as the human resources officer for my employer, I often find people who have lost hope. They have lost hope in their careers, they have lost hope in their relationships, and they have lost hope in their life goals. As I talk to these people and look for some way to help, I am reminded again and again of Rick Snyder and his Hope Theory. In its simplest form, Dr. Snyder taught that hope consisted of three elements illustrated in the diagram below from his book, *Handbook of Hope* (p. 10).

$$A \Rightarrow B$$

The person (**A**) perceives himself as being capable of producing a route or a pathway (**the arrow**) to a desired goal (**B**).

All three elements are necessary for people to maintain a hopeful position in life. To have hope, we need to have a goal, we need to believe we can attain the goal, and we need to see a way – a pathway – to attain it.

It occurred to me that this simple model is one way I can both identify what is holding people back and then recommend ways to help them regain the hope they have lost. For example, I met with a young woman whose life had taken a very difficult turn. She was devastated and hopeless. I remember telling her that I was

69

confident that she would be happy again and that her future could be very bright. I also remember that she gave me a look of profound disbelief. While I think she desperately wanted to be happy again, she didn't believe she could attain it and certainly could not see any pathways to get there.

Figure 8: One pathway blocked, another open

Over the weeks and months that we met she began to see options for moving forward. She identified her strengths and interests and pursued them. She began to cultivate a vision of her future. As she did this, her confidence also grew. I could see the elements of hope return and work together. The change in her was obvious, even in the way she walked. It was truly inspiring to watch hope return to my friend's life.

I discovered that if we could help people identify which of the three elements of hope they were missing, we could then identify remedies to get them back on track. Some people have no goals. Some people have no confidence or motivation. Others may have goals and confidence, but can't quite figure out where to take the first step. Sometimes one pathway gets blocked, and they need help figuring another way to move towards their goals.

There are various exercises and interventions to help establish (or re-establish) these hope elements. I ask people to envision their best possible future selves to gain a renewed vision of their potential, thereby increasing confidence in their ability to achieve their goals. I use the simple "SMART" model of goal-setting to help people set practical goals that are specific, measurable, aligned with their values, realistic, and time bound. I like to use simple brainstorming or mind-mapping techniques to help people create multiple options and pathways to bridge their motivation to their goals.

It's hard to imagine anyone being truly happy without also being hopeful. It's hard to imagine anyone who is truly hopeful without also being happy. I think they are inseparably connected. I have found that Dr. Snyder's model of hope provides multiple pathways to help those we care about.

Five Actions to Build Hope

by Tayyab Rashid

1. Recall a situation when you or someone close to you overcame a difficult obstacle and succeeded. Remember this precedent when you are faced with a similar situation.

2. Visualize where and what you want to be after one, five and ten years. Sketch a pathway that you can follow to get there. Include manageable steps and ways to chart your progress.

3. Recall bad decisions you made, forgive yourself, and see how you can make better decisions in the future. Learn from your mistakes rather than being haunted by them.

4. When facing adversity, focus on how you overcame a similar adversity in the past. Let your successes set the precedent for your future endeavors.

5. Surround yourself with optimistic and future-minded friends, particularly when you face a setback. Accept their encouragement and help, and let them know that you will do the same for them when they face obstacles.

Saint Joan (Monologue)

by Bernard Shaw

Read aloud to explore the strength of hope.

Joan: Where would I have been now if I had heeded that sort of truth? There is no help, no counsel, in any of you. Yes: I am alone on earth: I have always been alone. My father told my brothers to drown me if I would not stay to mind his sheep while France was bleeding to death: France might perish if only our lambs were safe. I thought France would have friends at the court of the king of France; and I find only wolves fighting for pieces of her poor torn body. I thought God would have friends everywhere, because He is the friend of everyone; and in my innocence I believed that you who now cast me out would be like strong towers to keep harm from me. But I am wiser now; and nobody is any the worse for being wiser. Do not think you can frighten me by telling me that I am alone. France is alone; and God is alone; and what is my loneliness before the loneliness of my country and my God? I see now that the loneliness of God is His strength: what would He be if he listened to your jealous little counsels? Well, my loneliness shall be my strength too; it is better to be alone with God: His friendship will not fail me, nor His counsel, nor His love. In His strength I will dare, and dare, and dare, until I die. I will go out now to the common people, and let the love in their eyes comfort me for the hate in yours. You will all be glad to see me burnt; but if I go through the fire I shall go through it to their hearts for ever and ever. And so, God be with me!

Humility

Humility and modesty represent the ability to forget oneself, to be content out of the center of the stage, to assess one's own mistakes and imperfections accurately, to be open to influence from others, and to put the needs of the group ahead of one's personal needs. CSV-462-463.

Becoming Unselved: The Mystery of Humility

by Kathryn Britton

What would you think if your top character strength were humility? A friend found it rather deflating. Humility sounds so ... unexciting. However, when we explored it together, we discovered that she had a great knack for taking herself out of the middle of the picture and focusing on the needs and behaviors of the people around her. Suddenly humility snapped into place as a quality that fit and that seemed a valuable part of herself.

June Price Tangney at George Mason University, describes humility as a rich, multi-faceted construct characterized by the following qualities:

- An accurate assessment of oneself, including both strengths and weaknesses — neither unduly favorable nor unduly unfavorable
- An openness to new information, including ideas that contradict former opinions
- An ability to keep one's own place in the world in perspective. Humble people are less inclined than the normal population to self-serving biases.
- An ability to forget oneself, to move out of the middle of the frame

Where does humility come from? Some research shows that humility probably arises from a sense of security grounded on feelings of self-worth that come from stable and reliable sources such as feeling unconditionally loved, sources that make a firmer foundation than many external sources, such as achievement, appearance, or social approval.

It was a bit of a surprise to me that humble people may be more firmly grounded in life than others.

What is humility good for? After working on humility for several years, Benjamin Franklin noticed that conversations with others were more pleasant, other people were more likely to listen to his opinions, and he had an easier time recovering when his opinions turned out to be wrong.

Figure 9: Put the spotlight on someone else

Management researcher Jim Collins argues that a key ingredient for moving from good to great is having leadership that combines humility with a fierce will. Leaders express humility by routinely crediting others for their organization's success while accepting personal blame when results are poor. They appear calm and determined, and they can subjugate their egos to the needs of the organization. In my experience, it can be surprising and inspiring to work for a humble leader.

Who has humility? Extensive interviews of adolescents found that humility, especially openness to other points of view, was associated with teens that had a strong sense of purpose. Here is a quotation from one of the interviewed teens:

"I think a core belief is that you can't do anything by yourself. Or anything that you think you do by yourself is really supported by a mountain of other people... I just think you really can never take personal credit for anything. That there are so many other things that go into that."

Humble individuals are less driven to impress and dominate others, and they tend to be less driven to collect special benefits for themselves. They experience a different benefit, being free from self-preoccupation. After all, the need to maintain an inflated self-image can be a psychological burden.

How can we build humility? Benjamin Franklin worked for years on humility especially in his conversational habits. For example, he denied himself the pleasure of contradicting other people, and he avoided words that implied fixed opinions. These habits became easier with long practice. He did admit that it was easier to achieve the appearance of humility than the fact. Pride is so hard to overcome, he stated, that "even if I could conceive that I had completely overcome it, I should probably be proud of my humility."

Children learn humility by observing role models among parents, teachers, community leaders, or heroes. Who are the heroes of humility? Benjamin Franklin because of his life-long effort and his accurate self-appraisal? Beth in *Little Women*, who avoided attention as she quietly served others? Mother Teresa who turned focus away from herself toward the people she served? The founders of Alcoholics Anonymous, whose 12-step program incorporates elements of humility such as admitting personal limitations? It can be hard to find exemplars of humility because they don't seek attention.

To build humility, we can practice behaviors that make us more aware of our indebtedness to other people, such as writing down those things for which we are grateful or seeking forgiveness. Seeking reliable attachments may be another approach, since the resulting psychological safety may be a critical enabling condition for humility.

Now that I've explored humility, I hold it in awe.

> *I have done one braver thing*
> *Than all the Worthies did*
> *Yet a braver thence doth spring*
> *Which is, to keepe that hid.*
> *~John Donne*

Five Actions to Build Humility

by Tayyab Rashid

1. Resist showing off accomplishments for a week and notice the changes in your interpersonal relationships. Do people act surprised that you waited to reveal your news?
2. Resist showing off if you notice that you are better than someone at some task. Allow others to notice your skills on their own.
3. Resist showing off when others shows off. Observe the reactions that show-offs get from observers.
4. Notice if you speak more than others in a group situation. Concentrate on listening to the words of others rather than simply waiting for your turn to speak.
5. Compliment sincerely if you find someone is authentic and better than you in some ways. Accept compliments from others humbly.

Nobel Peace Prize Speech (Excerpt)

by Mother Teresa

Read aloud to explore the strength of humility.

One evening we went out and we picked up four people from the street. And one of them was in a most terrible condition and I told the Sisters: You take care of the other three. I take of this one that looked worse. So I did for her all that my love can do. I put her in bed, and there was such a beautiful smile on her face. She took hold of my hand, as she said one word only: "Thank you," and she died.

I could not help but examine my conscience before her, and I asked what would I say if I was in her place. And my answer was very simple. I would have tried to draw a little attention to myself, I would have said I am hungry, that I am dying, I am cold, I am in pain, or something, but she gave me much more, she gave me her grateful love. And she died with a smile on her face. As that man whom we picked up from the drain, half eaten with worms, and we brought him to the home. "I have lived like an animal in the street, but I am going to die like an angel, loved and cared for." And it was so wonderful to see the greatness of that man who could speak like that, who could die like that without blaming anybody, without cursing anybody, without comparing anything. Like an angel this is the greatness of our people.

Humor

Humor as a character strength includes a playful recognition and enjoyment of the incongruities of life, the ability to see the light side of adversity, and the ability to make others smile and laugh. CSV-584-585

The Lighter Side of Life

by Homaira Kabir

"Laugh loudly, laugh often, laugh at yourself."
~ Chelsea Handler

My paternal grandmother was known for her infectious sense of humor. It is rumored that when she was young, her peals of laughter rang in the streets of her little neighborhood. She lived with us when I was growing up, and I remember her as my constant partner in mirth. She connected to my childlike sense of humor as naturally as she did to grown-up wit. When my husband-to-be proposed to me years later, she was a strong advocate for the match. Her conviction was based on the fact that he laughed a lot, hence would keep me happy.

Though illiterate, Dadima had a sharp insight into the workings of the mind. Decades later, I now study through science what she believed through intuition. From calming the cardiovascular system and improving depressive symptoms, to enhancing relationships and providing a greater purpose in life, humor is a primary contributor to a well-lived life.

Research shows humor to be an indispensable trait for effective leadership, not only as a de-stressor in challenging times but also as a promoter of workplace morale. Even being a parent is less bumpy when humor joins the ride. Mothers with cheery dispositions are able to move through the flow of family chaos in a stable manner, thus contributing to the development of a secure attachment in their children. Marriages are shown to be stronger when partners can appreciate the lighter side of life.

Other studies have demonstrated the effects of humor on recovery from bereavement. Humor may help individuals find perspective on their loss thus leading to less depression and a greater purpose in life. Certain therapy models, such as laughter yoga, encourage laughter to calm the stress response and perhaps even lead to a mystical experience of transcendence.

Figure 10: Laugh heartily

The centrality of humor in our lives is reflected in the ritualized roles within societies of jesters and comedians. Across time and cultures, making people laugh has played an important part in society, from the YuSze of imperial China to the court jesters of medieval Europe, from the stupidus of ancient Rome to the stand-ups in improv comedy clubs today.

Yet, while intended to make people laugh, humor can also bring tears of irritation or outbursts of anger. I am a regular witness to my daughter's desperate cries for help over her teenage brother's ideas of jokes. What is it about humor that can give rise to the most extreme form of moral emotions, from empathy and compassion to fury and contempt?

The answer may lie in the evolution of humor itself. Although even non-human primates engaged in social play, it was with the development of language that humans began to enjoy laughing and telling jokes. Humor is likely the result of a profound transition in the evolution of the brain, the emergence of consciousness.

Consciousness allowed us to create a coherent narrative of our history, with a lived past and an anticipated future. With the ability to look into the future came the realization of impending dangers and our eventual demise. This not only infused life with fear, it also created the desire to beat biological existence and find meaning by belonging to something more eternal than the finite self. Meaning provided the stability that the emotional upheaval of life did not, and humor allowed us to move past the chaos of constant change by focusing on the larger perspective and seeing the absurdity of most of our insignificant worries.

With consciousness too emerged the self that existed within the framework of other people. Morality and culture evolved to allow for peaceful coexistence within the social structures that were key to our survival. Humor built relationships within tribes and strengthened in-group bonds, often at the expense of inter-group relationships.

Today, however, our tribe is slightly larger than the couple of hundred people in our ancestors' times. We live a global existence, and our sense of humor has to take the sensitivities and cultures of 7 billion people into account if we are indeed to thrive as humanity. This is not always easy, and yet it is essential.

So what are we to do? Laughing at another's expense disconnects us from our human values.

In our interconnected world, we need to build other-focused strengths that take all cultures and traditions into account. To build empathy, we need to connect our own individual experience with another's pain and expose ourselves to other cultural experiences.

Perhaps the focus on the other will also help my son develop his budding career. I may remind my young comedian that a joke ceases to be a joke when it offends the sensitivities of the person who witnesses it, and that the success of any stand-up depends on his ability to refine an effective act that is appropriate for different audiences in different settings, depending on tastes, traits and temperament. Strutting around with boxers over his head or socks hanging off his ears may not be the most appropriate form of humor when his twin sister is trying to solve a complicated math equation. Until he manages to build social intelligence and a more coherent act, I may warn him to simply stop when he finds that the other person is not laughing with him. Trying to clarify his humor can lead to the most desperate cries for help. E. B. White, the great New Yorker humorist, once observed that explaining humor is a bit like dissecting a frog: "It can be done, but the subject tends to die in the process." I may also help my daughter build her own sense of humor by encouraging her to nurture her imagination. I may remind her of her contagious peals of laughter at her brother's attempts at comedy not too long ago, and how they enhanced both their happiness and their relationship. Enabling her to appreciate the absurd and the unexpected will undoubtedly fuel her imagination and contribute to her growth.

At the end of the day, all we want is to be happy and live meaningful lives. Although life may simply be a meaningless ride that we try and cloak with a fulfilling purpose, humor allows us to laugh at the insignificance of most things in the vast flow of human experience and yet connect to what we find truly important.

Our memories of Dadima are filled with the smiles she spread. Her instincts about my husband were right for he fills our days with much laughter and joy. In life and after death, we will be known for the way we make others feel. Happy beats unhappy any day.

Five Actions to Build Humor

by Tayyab Rashid

1. Find the fun and lighter side in most situations. Strike a balance between taking things seriously enough and not taking them too seriously.
2. Learn a new joke three times a week and tell them to friends. Note how laughing together improves the mood of the group.
3. Be friends with someone who has a great sense of humor. Watch how they use this strength to deal with difficult situations and bad news.
4. Go out with your friends at least once a month for bowling, hiking, cross-country skiing, biking, and such. Note how the group dynamic improves when you laugh together.
5. Send funny emails to your friends. Rather than simply forwarding chain letters, share humor from your own life.

The Importance of Being Earnest (Monologue)

by Oscar Wilde

Read aloud to explore the strength of humor.

Lady Bracknell: Well, I must say, Algernon, that I think it is high time that Mr. Bunbury made up his mind whether he was going to live or die. This shilly-shallying with the question is absurd. Nor do I in any way approve of the modern sympathy with invalids. I consider it morbid. Illness of any kind is hardly a thing to be encouraged in others. Health is the primary duty of life. I am always telling that to your poor uncle, but he never seems to take much notice . . . as far as any improvement in his ailment goes. I should be much obliged if you would ask Mr. Bunbury, from me, to be kind enough not to have a relapse on Saturday, for I rely on you to arrange my music for me. It is my last reception, and one wants something that will encourage conversation, particularly at the end of the season when everyone has practically said whatever they had to say, which, in most cases, was probably not much.

Integrity

"Integrity, authenticity, and honesty capture a character trait in which people are true to themselves, accurately representing – privately and publicly – their internal states, intentions, and commitments." This character strength involves both truthfulness and taking responsibility for one's actions, emotions, and thoughts. People with integrity do the right thing according to their own inner lights even when it is not easy. CSV-249-250.

Comfortable in Your Own Skin

by Jan Stanley

When temperatures drop with the coming of autumn, I love wrapping up in my most comfortable warm wool sweaters. A favorite is my fine gauge taupe cardigan with the gold buttons. It looks, smells, and feels like genuine wool. If I had a microscope handy, I could see wool down to its smallest visible fibers. What about ourselves? What can we say about ourselves that is true in every fiber of our beings?

There is a character strength that belongs to people who are who they say they are, through and through, like my wool sweater. This strength comprises 3 slightly different traits:

Integrity means living up to the commitments or standards set for oneself, being a "person of his or her word."

Honesty is being centered on the truth in words and in actions.

Authenticity is living one's values and beliefs, being true to oneself and expressing that truth to the outside world. There is little facade or pretense when people with authenticity express themselves, and we find ourselves drawn to them because of it.

I am most intrigued by authenticity. Even though it is a valued strength across time, geography, and cultures, empirical research on it, especially as it relates to well-being, has lagged

87

behind research on other strengths such as gratitude, hope, and optimism. This is beginning to change, and that is a good thing, because authenticity plays a key role in our well-being.

Figure 11: Every fiber is real.

One research study introduced an authenticity scale along with findings that demonstrate connections between authenticity and well-being. The assessment includes self-report questions such as, "I think it is better to be yourself than to be popular," and "I always stand by what I believe in." After refinement, the researchers narrowed the assessment to twelve questions defining authenticity in a way that could be divided into three subscales: authentic living, how much people accept external influence, and how much they feel alienated from themselves.

Subscale One: Authentic Living: Authentic living correlated positively with happiness. When we have the courage to live authentically, we feel better! This is an example of research catching up with wisdom through the ages. As one case in point, see how Polonius' advice to Laertes in Shakespeare's Hamlet reflects authentic living.

"This above all: to thine own self be true,
And it must follow, as the night the day,
Thou canst not then be false to any man."

Were he writing it today, with the advantage of this new research, Shakespeare might have added a fourth line, something like, "..... And thine well-being will shine as a star bright in the northern skies!"

Subscale Two: Accepting External Influence is measuring the degree to which we conform to others' suggestions or expectations. External influence includes conforming broadly to societal expectations, or the more targeted receptivity to loved ones' expectations of us. Accepting external influence was associated with a decline in psychological well-being and with increases in stress.

This has been true in my own life. After having made a firm but difficult decision to transition careers many years ago, I accepted a position from a friend in need who convinced me that my knowledge and skills would contribute to a worthy cause. I signed a 1-year agreement, even though it was in conflict with the direction I had set for myself. Accepting this external influence amplified my stress, which created serious health impacts for me. It made me less effective in the role than I might have been, had I been more authentically aligned with it.

Subscale Three: Self-Alienation is almost the opposite of authenticity. High scores on these questions were associated with much higher levels of stress and anxiety and lower levels of well-being. It follows that we can improve well-being by identifying and removing ways that we alienate ourselves from our beliefs or ideals. While not all stress is caused by self-alienation, this study suggests that looking for ways we can be more aligned with our values, ideals, and images of our true selves is a route to greater well-being.

Let's think about the cost of self-alienation using an example from the *Dead Poets' Society*. The decision of Mr. Keating (played by Robin Williams) to maintain his authenticity cost him his job at Welton Academy. Who can forget the scene where the boys, led by Todd, who had struggled to find his own authentic voice, stand on their desks calling out, "O Captain! My Captain!" as Mr. Keating leaves the classroom for the last time? The cost of staying true to himself was seemingly very high. In contrast, we can only speculate about the cost if Mr. Keating had acquiesced, teaching for his remaining decades in a way that was self-alienating. He might have led what Thoreau described as a life of "quiet desperation."

Living authentically comes naturally to some for whom it is a signature strength. For others, more thought and action may be required to ramp up authenticity. Here are three evidence-based approaches to consider.

Avenue 1: Use Mindfulness and Curiosity: The term "beginner's mind" is sometimes used when learning mindfulness meditation. It means bringing fresh eyes to familiar things, as if seeing them for the first time, even something as common as the raisin that is often used in teaching this skill. What if we bring this powerful tool of beginner's mind to our own selves, seeing ourselves as if for the first time?

Given that authenticity is how closely we express our true selves to the world, we can use mindfulness and curiosity to close the gap between our ideal and actual selves.

Avenue 2: Understand Your Motivations: External influences can decrease our well-being and increase our experienced stress. A first step is to know the difference between our own motivations and external motivations. Well-being increases when the value of extrinsic motivators like popularity, image, and financial success are reduced in our lives.

So as you reflect on the ways you spend your time and energy, ask yourself whether your motivation is coming from within. If your values line up too heavily on the materialistic side, you may choose to make life changes that align more closely with your inner values and goals.

Avenue 3: Reflect on Your Life: Reflection on personal values and beliefs may influence authenticity, too. In one study, each participant selected two meaningful personal intrinsic values and then received weekly emails for a month reminding them of their chosen values along with supporting quotations and messages.

Each participant was also asked to reflect on personal values. Well-being increased immediately. Four weeks later, extrinsic motivators had decreased while intrinsic motivation and well-being had increased. The more engaged participants were in self-reflection, the greater their extrinsic values declined and the more their well-being improved.

Perhaps reflecting on our motivations amplifies that little voice in our minds that seems to be able to connect us with our true selves, thereby enhancing our well-being.

Mindfulness, assessing our motivations, and reflecting on our lives may seem like a great deal of difficult work. Why pursue it? Why now, when we've lived a significant portion of our lives already? There are several important reasons, in addition to enhanced well-being.

Improved Relationships: Think about someone who lacks authenticity. You might describe them as deceitful or dishonest, maybe even as a poser or a phony. These aren't the people most of us would like to get to know. The more authentically we live, the more likely we are to receive social benefits such as being well liked, supported by friends, and participating collaboratively with others.

Increased Vitality: When people act on intrinsic motivation, vitality either remains stable or is enhanced.

Vitality is correlated with many good things, including performance, perseverance, and well-being. When we act on our own motivations and not the influence or expectations of others, we live more authentically, and we feel alive!

No Regrets: An Australian hospice nurse named Bronnie Ware categorized regrets expressed by dying patients. She spent time with her patients in their final weeks of life, as they received palliative care in the comfort of their own homes. Ware reports that the most common regret was, "I wish I'd had the courage to live a life true to myself, not the life others expected of me."

If you are able to read this article, there is still time to act. What courageous actions could you take to live your life more authentically? Like a sweater that is wool through and through, be true to yourself.

Five Actions to Build Integrity

by Tayyab Rashid

1. Monitor every time you tell a lie, even if it is a small one. Try to make your list shorter every day.

2. Monitor to catch lies of omission (such as not volunteering important information when selling a used item) and think how you would feel if someone did the same to you. Try to be forthcoming in your dealings with others.

3. Think and act fairly when you face your next challenge, regardless of its impact on your position or popularity. Put aside your perceptions of peer pressure when making your decision.

4. Monitor whether your next five significant actions match your words and vice-versa. Try to act in a manner that is consistent with what you say.

5. Identify your area of strongest moral convictions. Set your long-term priorities according to these convictions.

Chief Sitting Bull (Speech)

Read aloud to explore the strength of integrity.

It doesn't interest me what you do for a living. I want to know what you ache for.

It doesn't interest me how old you are. I want to know if you will risk looking like a fool for love.

It doesn't interest me how much money you make. I want to know if you have touched the center of your soul.

It doesn't interest me if the story you're telling me is true. I want to know if you can disappoint another to be true to yourself.

I want to know if you can be faithful and therefore trustworthy.

I want to know if you can see beauty even if it is not pretty every day.

I want to know if you can live with failure...yours and mine.

I want to know if you can get up after a night of grief and despair and do what needs to be done.

I want to know if you will stand in the center of the fire with me and not shrink back.

Kindness

"Kindness and altruistic love require the assertion of a common humanity in which others are worthy of attention and affirmation for no utilitarian reasons but for their own sake." Kindness has an emotional grounding that makes it more than duty. This emotional grounding leads to awareness of the needs of others and willingness to supply those needs without expecting a return. CSV-326

Halfhearted or Wholehearted Helper?

by Bridget Grenville-Cleave

Even simple acts of kindness, such as holding the door open for a stranger or helping someone carry groceries to the car, can increase well-being, particularly if you do them in concentrated bursts. Perhaps being kind makes us happier by increasing self-regard, creating positive social interactions, and increasing charitable feelings towards others. Acts of kindness improve the quality of relationships.

During my MAPP studies at the University of East London, a small group in my class decided to do our own pseudo-experiment with random acts of kindness. One Saturday evening we set about distributing bottles of Budweiser which were left over from our faculty summer party to other students, some that we passed on the way back to our residence hall, some waiting at the campus bus stop for a ride into town, some diligently doing their washing in the campus launderette. Of course we couldn't measure the effect scientifically, but we definitely felt good giving our stuff away, and judging by the smiles, amusement, and gratitude, the people given bottles of Budweiser for free also felt good. For some it looked like the very first time they'd been given something for nothing. We had to assure them it wasn't a trick and they weren't on the old TV show, *Candid Camera*.

95

Netta Weinstein and Richard Ryan have studied the impact of doing things for others. They looked at the link between well-being and *autonomous help* on the one hand versus *controlled help* on the other hand. With autonomous help, we freely give because we want to help. With controlled help, we're coerced into giving, perhaps because we feel guilty or because we're told to help or because we get some reward for helping. They set up ways to measure autonomous help and gave instructions that resulted in controlled help.

Figure 12: Share freely

What is perhaps surprising is that helping others, per se, did not generally relate to well-being as measured by subjective well-being, vitality, or self-esteem. People who engaged in more controlled helpful behaviors across the 2 weeks were not better off, nor were people better off on days when they helped someone compared to days when they did not. Yet autonomous help had a consistent and substantial impact on well-being.

These studies suggest that it may not be the helping act itself that is responsible for increasing the well-being of the helper, but rather the motivation for the act. This is an important clarification of the general message that helping is good for your well-being.

Did well-being increase for the people being helped? Recipients of autonomous help experienced higher well-being, whereas recipients of controlled help didn't get any well-being benefits. Some even reported *lower* well-being than those who didn't receive any help at all! Recipients of autonomous help thought that their helpers made more effort, and they felt closer to them.

It's worth pointing out that in the study, the people who received help weren't told their helper's motivation. The researchers suggest that therefore their responses were generated entirely as a result of the quality of the interpersonal experience. Thus receiving autonomous help makes you feel more valued, compared to receiving help that the helper feels compelled to give. I'm not so sure about this explanation. Personally I think it's quite likely that at least some of the people could instinctively detect the motivation of the helper.

Nevertheless, this research does raise some interesting questions about the impact of your helping on the well-being of other people, particularly when having no choice as to whether you help or not seems to result in their well-being being lower than if you didn't help them in the first place. So perhaps we all need to think twice before we do things for others halfheartedly or begrudgingly. The research seems to suggest either to help wholeheartedly, or not at all.

Five Actions to Build Kindness

by Tayyab Rashid

1. Do three random acts of kindness per week for those whom you know. Consider doing small favors for friends and neighbors, calling sick or sad friends, getting groceries for a friend busy in exams, cooking a meal for an elderly relative, or baby-sitting.

2. Say kinder and softer words to people when interacting through email, writing letters, talking on phone. Be aware that communication over distance requires different types of gentleness than face-to-face communication.

3. Share your belongings with others (e.g., lawn mower, snow blower, jumper cables). Offer to help them if they don't know how to operate equipment or go about accomplishing a task.

4. While driving, give way to others and be courteous of pedestrians and bicyclists. When entering or exiting buildings, hold the door for others.

5. Help fix someone's flat tire or offer your cell phone to a stranded motorist. Carry jumper cables and flares in your trunk in case you need to help someone on the road.

Bob Hope Humanitarian Award (Speech)

by Oprah Winfrey

Read aloud to explore the strength of kindness.

I grew up in Nashville with a father who owned a barbershop, Winfrey's Barber Shop, he still does, I can't get him to retire. And every holiday, *every* holiday, all of the transients and the guys who I thought were just losers who hung out at the shop, and were always bumming haircuts from my father and borrowing money from my dad, all those guys always ended up at our dinner table. They were a cast of real characters—it was Fox and Shorty and Bootsy and Slim. And I would say, "Bootsy, could you pass the peas please?" And I would often say to my father afterwards, "Dad, why can't we just have regular people at our Christmas dinner?" because I was looking for the Currier & Ives version. And my father said to me, "They are regular people. They're just like you. They want the same thing you want." And I would say, "What?" And he'd say, "To be fed." And at the time, I just thought he was talking about dinner. But I have since learned how profound he really was, because we all are just regular people seeking the same thing. The guy on the street, the woman in the classroom, the Israeli, the Afghani, the Zuni, the Apache, the Irish, the Protestant, the Catholic, the gay, the straight, you, me— we all just want to know that we matter. We want validation. We want the same things. We want safety and we want to live a long life. We want to find somebody to love. [...] We want to find somebody to laugh with and have the power and the place to cry with when necessary.

The greatest pain in life is to be invisible. What I've learned is that we all just want to be heard. And I thank all the people who continue to let me hear your stories, and by sharing your stories, you let other people see themselves and for a moment, glimpse the power to change and the power to triumph. Maya Angelou said, 'When you learn, teach. When you get, give.' I want you to

99

know that this award to me means that I will continue to strive to give back to the world what it has given to me, so that I might even be more worthy of tonight's honor. Thank you.

Leadership

Leadership involves directing group activities toward collective success, creating good relationships among group members, and preserving morale. "Leadership is fulfilling when done well. Setting goals and accomplishing them, enlisting effective help, building coalitions, smoothing ruffled feathers..." CSV-365, CSV-414

Interview with Tom Rath

by Margaret Greenberg

Love in a business book? I think you will be surprised by the ways that love shows up the book by Tom Rath and Barry Conchie called *Strengths Based Leadership: Great Leaders, Teams, and Why People Follow*. What differentiates this book is the new research on what followers need from the leaders in their lives. Four clear themes emerged: trust, compassion, stability, and hope.

I interviewed Tom Rath to explore what he knows about leadership.

Margaret: What would you say are the biggest take-away messages from this book?

Tom: From earlier research, we know great leaders never need to be well rounded, but great teams probably do. The three main messages of this book are:

1. You need to know your individual strengths.
2. You need to have the right people on your team and understand the strengths of the people around you.
3. You need to meet your followers' needs. That is the new research in the book: what followers need from leaders.

Margaret: In the book you write, "You're a leader of an organization if others follow." Typically when we study leadership, we interview leaders to get their opinions on what they do. Rarely do we solicit the opinions of followers the way you did in this book. Tell me more.

Tom: We often glaze over the fact that leaders need followers, and the person who has the best vantage point to judge if a leader makes a difference or not is the individual who is following. We asked 20,000 people from around the world to think of a leader that had the most impact in their life. Then in a very open-ended way and in their own words, we asked them why they follow. We then sorted and coded their responses.

Figure 13: Lead like a shepherd

Margaret: What was the most surprising finding?

Tom: I was surprised by what wasn't at the top of the list. We didn't see followers talking about vision, clarity, or purpose. The irony is that is what the literature talks about most of the time. Leaders do need to think about where the company is going strategically, but there are basic things they need to do on a regular basis to maintain relationships.

Margaret: What else surprised you?

Tom: The other finding we didn't spend much time on in book is the median duration of the relationship between a follower and the person that had the most impact on their daily life. It was ten years. That kind of leadership takes place within the context of a really powerful relationship. Leaders need to keep in mind that having that kind influence and building that kind of relationship with 5 or 500 takes a lot of time and patience.

Margaret: What about the "L" word — love? Did people use that word when describing the leader that had the most impact?

Tom: People did use the word *love* quite frequently, along with caring and compassion when talking about great local leaders like mentors, managers, spouses, parents, and teachers. The word speaks to just how close these relationships are. When we asked about organizational and global leaders that had the most impact, people used words like *caring* and *compassion.*

I've learned that the word love is a lightning rod in organizations. The word makes people uncomfortable. The way love manifests itself in business specifically is in managers who care. Gallup has collected research on the topic of caring managers. We've asked 15 million people, "Does your manager care about you as a person?" Not only do the very best managers have employees who say they care, but the managers themselves see the development of their people as being an end in itself, versus a means to another end.

Margaret: You describe four leadership domains: Executing, Influencing, Relationship Building, and Strategic Thinking, and then you illustrate each domain by interviewing highly successful organizational leaders. Tell me more.

Tom: I have admired the people I interviewed for a long time, and they were just night and day different in the way they interacted with people and built their organizations. From the minute I sat down with Wendy Kopp (Founder and CEO of Teach for America) she oozed achievement. She guided me through how she methodically worked on her to-do list from day, to week, to month, to year until she had built that organization essentially from scratch. Within 12 months of writing her thesis she was on the front page of the New York Times, recruited 500 teachers in California, and raised over $2.5 million. I'm still blown away by that.

But the interview that was really striking for me was Mervyn Davies (Chairman of Standard Chartered Bank). When you think of a chairman of a large global bank in the UK you don't think of a guy that leads with relationships. He talked about how the well-being of 70,000 families depends on the company. I interviewed some of his direct reports and they described how Mervyn was there for them when they had a real personal challenge. To build a global bank like that and do it all through a pretty heavy relationship orientation was really neat to see.

Margaret: Did you find common strengths among leaders?

Tom: No. That's been one of the big takeaways for me. We don't see much of any consistency when we look at the most successful leaders. I've yet to see two that have a very similar profile in terms of their top 5 strengths.

Margaret: One question I am frequently asked by leaders is, "How can we get employees to think beyond their department and collaborate more with other areas in order to better execute and get the work done?" How would you answer that question?

Tom: It might sound somewhat elementary, but just do some basic things to ensure people are talking. I know this doesn't happen anywhere near as much as it should, but just sit down, ideally face-to-face, and get to know the people that you're going to be interfacing with on a regular basis. Spend a little bit of time talking about their strengths so they know that what each can contribute is important. I'm amazed at how often teams are formed, and that just doesn't take place at all. Companies should see the value in doing that, if for no other reason than for the sake of speed. For example, I have five close relationships here at work.

I can communicate something to them, or they can communicate to me, in 10 or 15 seconds versus 10 or 15 minutes it would take if I didn't have that close relationship.

Margaret: It would be interesting to look at a team's make-up and see if they have any Relationship Building strengths. Maybe that plays into how collaborative people will be?

Tom: It's a great point. A lot of the top leadership teams we've worked with have been most thin in the area of Relationship Building. I know that I thought about that a lot a couple of years ago with my own team. I have someone on my team who is ten times better than I ever will be at keeping us cohesive and building relationships. So I said to her explicitly, "I may be the one managing the team, but I know you're better at doing this." She's done so much to help us build a better environment with an even broader group of people.

Margaret: Now what are you working on?

Tom: We're doing a lot of work trying to connect how engaged employees are on the job and when people have a chance to use their strengths, how that relates to outcomes that are more about one's own physical health. We have a few experiments underway where we've been looking at when people become more engaged in their jobs, what happens to their total cholesterol levels, the triglyceride in their bloodstream, and their cortisol or stress hormone levels. As much as productivity, profitability, customer scores, and turnover are important to organizations, and I'd call those hard or concrete metrics for companies, I think that our physical health is one means to look at pretty concrete outcomes for individuals.

Margaret: For the company it would translate into health care costs, which continue to be one of the largest expenses for most companies.

Tom: I think that's a big part of it. We're trying to figure out exactly how much of the variance of health care costs that individual engagement accounts for. A lot of good companies like

Standard Chartered mentioned earlier, will get to the point where they care about it for all the right reasons and the rest of the companies will get there for no other reason than they'll see the reduction in health care costs. The more we dive into the research we're collecting, the more it seems that the quality of people's managers is a better predictor of overall health than the quality of their physicians.

Margaret: Many people are surprised when I tell them that your grandfather, Donald Clifton, wrote *Now, Discover Your Strengths*. What do you think your grandfather would have to say about your latest book?

Tom: Right before he passed away he sent an e-mail summarizing some of his best thoughts on the topic of leadership. He typed a long note describing some of his key findings. That note was probably the best outline and skeleton that served to guide us as we were working on this book. He had done so much research over the years and had a lot of good thoughts that just never quite made it to publication in his lifetime. I'm sure he'd be glad to see the continuation of that work and to know that we've been able to help more people benefit from his work.

Five Actions to Build Leadership

by Tayyab Rashid

1. Organize a family event that is intergenerational, including both young and old relatives. Involve everyone in conversation rather than allowing age groups to self-segregate. Draw people's attention to cross-generational similarities.

2. Stand up for someone who is being treated unfairly. Encourage other leaders to emphasize fairness in their group processes.

3. Rotate leadership of an event or activity. Give others the chance to be leaders and speak with them about their experiences.

4. Read a biography and/or watch film of your favorite leader and evaluate how he/she inspires you in practical ways. Consider what strengths you share with this figure.

5. When two people are in an argument, mediate by inviting others to share their thoughts and emphasizing problem solving. Set a respectful, open-minded tone for the discussion.

We Choose to Go to the Moon (Excerpt)

by John Fitzgerald Kennedy, September 12, 1962

Read aloud to explore the strength of leadership.

No man can fully grasp how far and how fast we have come, but condense, if you will, the 50,000 years of man's recorded history in a time span of but a half a century. [...] About 10 years ago, under this standard, man emerged from his caves to construct other kinds of shelter. Only five years ago man learned to write and use a cart with wheels. [...] Last month electric lights and telephones and automobiles and airplanes became available. Only last week did we develop penicillin and television and nuclear power, and now if America's new spacecraft succeeds in reaching Venus, we will have literally reached the stars before midnight tonight.

William Bradford, speaking in 1630 of the founding of the Plymouth Bay Colony, said that all great and honorable actions are accompanied with great difficulties, and both must be enterprised and overcome with answerable courage. [...]

For the eyes of the world now look into space, to the moon and to the planets beyond, and we have vowed that we shall not see it governed by a hostile flag of conquest, but by a banner of freedom and peace. We have vowed that we shall not see space filled with weapons of mass destruction, but with instruments of knowledge and understanding.

We choose to go to the moon. We choose to go to the moon in this decade and do the other things, not because they are easy, but because they are hard, because that goal will serve to organize and measure the best of our energies and skills, because that challenge is one that we are willing to accept.

For the rest of the speech, go to *http://bit.ly/JFKMoonSpeech*

Love and Be Loved

Love takes three main forms: love for those that care and protect us, love for those we protect and care for, and love for a partner where we both make each other feel special. We can feel more than one form of love for an individual, and the form we feel can change over time. "Love is marked by the sharing of aid, comfort, and acceptance. It involves strong positive feelings, commitment, even sacrifice." CSV-293

How to Tell True Love from Ersatz Love

by George Vaillant

First, what is real love? To understand love, those usually helpful resources—the ancient Greeks, the poets, the psychologists, even Cupid—all fail us. Too readily, these experts become preoccupied with lust and forget about lasting attachment. The Buddha, too, lets us down, for he was too preoccupied with compassion to appreciate lasting attachment. Love is compassionate; but compassion is not always love. Real love is attached, selective, and enduring. In contrast, compassion does best when it is detached and rooted in time present. Mature mammalian, not just human, love involves enduring, remarkably unselfish attachment. Mate choice and bonding, if relatively involuntary, is driven by the altruistic, if still biological, motivation of oxytocin and mirror cells.

The Greek philosophers did not and the cognitive psychologists do not always understand attachment. The Greeks' agape (universal unselfish love) is not selective, and their Eros (testosterone, estrogen and all-about-me lust) is not enduring. Love, like the sacred and our image of God, has a timeless quality. The spirit behind the New Testament words, "God is love," can be found in even the self-consciously atheistic Great Soviet Encyclopedia, which explains to us "Love is the point at which the

109

opposing elements of the biological and the spiritual, the personal and the social, and the intimate and the universal intersect." Novelist Laurence Durrell reminds us, "The richest love is that which submits to the arbitration of time." In contrast, lust marches to a marvelous but much more urgent drummer. The object of a passionate one-night-stand may seem boring and ugly the next morning. But what a wonderful evening!

The Buddha feared attachment. He correctly saw it as the root of much sorrow. Welcome to the world of love. Love is dangerous. Indeed, for many of us, love, like joy, is sometimes difficult to bear. For love – like joy and gratitude – makes us feel vulnerable, sometimes so vulnerable that we are afraid to take love in, let alone give it back. What if your child died, or your sweetheart left you? In contrast, William Blake understood the importance of attachment, both its loss and its restoration. He reminds us, "Joy and grief are woven fine...Under every grief and pine runs a joy with silken twine." Savor lost loves. Don't just mourn them.

What is the difference between addiction and attachment? The lonely cynic sneers that "falling in love" is just another form of addiction. Attachment fueled by oxytocin is indeed, dangerous stuff; it makes you fall in love and never get over it. Don Juan and the Buddha had the right idea: Don't get attached! Consider Henry Higgins' lament: "I was serenely independent and content before we met; surely I could always be that way again—and yet... I've grown accustomed to her look; accustomed to her voice; accustomed to her face. Damn! Damn! Damn! Damn!" What is the difference between addiction and mammalian love?

Ah, let me count the ways. First, mammalian love is uniquely fueled by oxytocin and linked to limbic brain centers that are not linked to addiction. Admittedly, both addiction and love are fueled with the much less specific neurotransmitter dopamine. Dopamine, interestingly, is concentrated in brain centers that also contain opiate receptors. These centers are linked to heroin addiction—an ersatz and often lethal "love" that is also selective and enduring.

However, there is a second critical difference between heroin and love. Addiction is all about me, attachment all about the other. Addiction shouts, "Alack, poor me!" Love compassionately asks others, "Are you feeling better?"

Third, we rapidly habituate to our addictions. We need more and more for the same effect. In contrast, the soft touches of real love never stale.

Fourth, an addict in withdrawal is in a crisis of *sympathetic arousal*: fever, sweating, fast heart rate, high blood pressure, and irritable screams at anyone who tries to hug him. In contrast, a husband at his wife's gravesite is in a state of *parasympathetic withdrawal*: sobbing gently, slow pulse, grateful for a friend's arm around his shoulder. Grief over a loving attachment is in some ways still a positive emotion that in time helps us to broaden and build. Addiction destroys us physically, mentally, and spiritually.

Finally, "the morning after" is always the crucial test between true attachment and addiction. Mother bears are delighted by what they find cuddled up to them next morning; lusty participants in bacchanalias are less enthusiastic about what they find at dawn's early light.

Where does love come from? We do not learn how to love from religious education or from life coaching. Love does not come from the Buddha's mindfulness.

We learn love from our genes, from our biochemistry, and from the people who love us and who let us love them.

The brain hormone, oxytocin, is released when all mammals give birth. Oxytocin seems to permit mammals to overcome their natural aversion to extreme proximity; and, thus, oxytocin has been rechristened the "cuddle hormone." In human newborns, there is a short-lived overproduction of oxytocin. Oxytocin goes up in human puberty in parallel with adolescent crushes. Put a newborn baby in a mother's arms or bless a couple's sexual union with mutual orgasm and brain oxytocin levels rise. If they are genetically deprived of oxytocin, *prairie voles* (a species of rodent) that are normally monogamous, maternal, and loving turn into another subspecies—the heartless, promiscuous, pup-abusing *montane voles*. Without oxytocin, parental cooperation and responsibility vanishes.

Figure 14: Love matters.

But love is not just about genes and hormones. If, as the French planter sings in *South Pacific*, "You have to be taught to hate and fear," you also have to be shown how to love.

Love is about attachment, music, and odors; states that do not lend themselves to words. Song maybe, but not words. Thus, the behavioral self-regulation that we associate with love does not come from a solitary brain, but from one brain evolving and becoming shaped forever through attachment to a beloved other. Monkeys raised in isolation go on eating binges and cower in corners. Instead of playful roughhousing, they fight with their peers unto death, and they never really get the hang of copulation. All their lives such isolated monkeys remain inept "at doing what comes naturally."

In contrast, isolated monkeys who are subsequently raised by mothers or with siblings for even one year can learn to roughhouse—gracefully stopping once social dominance is achieved. They learn to skillfully negotiate the dance steps to successful impregnation.

In closing, I may do well to remind the reader that love songs, too, are for the transmission of love.

Mindful Love

by Kirsten Cronlund

Having a holiday dedicated completely to the savoring of romantic relationships seems a likely way to enhance and cultivate positive emotion, express gratitude, and even feel gratitude. I'm sure there are many who have lovely romantic Valentine's Day celebrations.

Yet even the most loving relationships go through ups and downs. Dedicating a holiday to highlighting romance and passion might cause stress for some people because we all fall victim to social comparison. It's easy to assume that everyone else is feeling close to his or her romantic partner and that there must be something wrong with our relationships if we are not lovey-dovey.

I'm not a cynic. So don't take it the wrong way when I say that romance is overrated. There's nothing wrong with you if your Valentine's Day is not Hallmark-worthy, and there may not even be anything wrong with your relationship if you would rather spend Valentine's Day by yourself soaking in a tub and reading a good novel, than getting dressed up and engaging in stimulating conversation with your spouse.

In her book, *Love 2.0*, Barbara Fredrickson defines love in terms of positivity resonance, a state of shared positive emotion, biochemical synchrony, and a shared motive to invest in each other's well-being. Maybe your way to express love is contained in the activities of daily life: actively responding to each other's good news, unloading the dishwasher, picking the children up from soccer practice, or painting the kitchen together. There's nothing wrong with this.

We can make ourselves supremely unhappy when we *maximize*, that is, search and search for the "perfect" object or decision. We set ourselves up for disappointment because the amount of time and energy we invest in this process makes us subconsciously expect a highly unlikely level of happiness with our final decision. This is true when researching for the best dishwasher, and it is also true in relationships. We are most happy when we set for ourselves a limited set of criteria for a good solution and quit looking when we have satisfied those requirements. It's best not to second-guess our decisions and to avoid comparisons to others as much as possible.

This advice is perhaps relatively easy to follow when buying a vacuum, but it's not so easy to remain as satisfied with one's spouse. Conflict is inherent in all relationships, and the complex negotiation involved in merging two outlooks and lifestyles incites people to periodically question whether or not they have made the right choice of spouse. It's easier said than done to set criteria for that choice and then not look back. It is possible, however, to achieve a great deal of contentment and peace with your spouse if you practice mindfulness in your relationship.

What does this look like? Mindfulness, attending nonjudgmentally to all stimuli in the external and internal environment, is perhaps the greatest pathway to satisfying relationships. When you raise awareness nonjudgmentally about your irritations over your spouse's spending habits, his or her need for more support with household chores, your mother-in-law's expectation about holiday traditions, and your conflicting ideas about ideal parenting practices, you can become a dispassionate observer of your inner and outer circumstances. "There's that irritation again," you might say to yourself, avoiding labeling it as "bad." Labeling it as bad activates the sympathetic nervous system to prepare for fight or flight.

Instead, as the observer, you are in a position to exercise the most effective optimistic approach, which is to scan the available options, determine the action that is most likely to yield positive results, and then take action. This mindful approach activates instead the parasympathetic nervous system, or the calming response. This leads to more shared positive moments.

What is the goal of this nonjudgmental scanning? The goal is not to erase the irritation, but to work with it to continue moving forward. Your irritation with your spouse is like the boulder in the path of a stream. Beating yourself against the boulder, either through angry expletives or through efforts to make him or her do what you want, will not yield positive results. Instead, you'll both continue to be stuck at that spot in the stream.

It might seem that this approach would lead to passivity in the relationship, but that is not what happens. People who engage in a mindful approach accurately assess the best ways to express their emotions, and when to do so. Conflict is not avoided, but navigated more successfully. Also, a clearer assessment of behaviors and dynamics leads to a greater chance that you will take action in unhealthy situations, such as your spouse spending the grocery money at the casino. The mindful approach also does not preclude the expression of joy and passion, but leads instead to unconditional love. But it does promote, most of all, contentment, a positive state that gets a bad rap in our culture. Contentment is a powerful emotion, and is associated with high levels of well-being.

Mindfulness makes space for shared positive emotions to occur. So I'd like to propose a mindful approach to Valentine's Day and love in general. Why not do what makes sense in your relationship? Maybe it's a dozen roses and a night of passionate lovemaking, but maybe it's an amiable chat or a few hours spent doing separate but meaningful activities. Most of all, excuse yourself of any expectations of the way love is supposed to be expressed.

Happiness Equals Love, Full Stop

by George Vaillant

In 2009, *The Atlantic* wrote an article summarizing a 70-year Harvard project, The Study of Adult Development. When I was interviewed as the director of the study for 40 years, I made two rash generalizations, "The only thing that really matters in life are your relationships to other people," and "Happiness equals love— full stop." Let me defend my seemingly sentimental generalizations about the findings of a multi-million dollar, seven-decade study designed to identify the key ingredients that lead to a good life.

When I praised relationships, was I speaking from my heart and not from science? In order to find out, I went back to the data. I reviewed the findings on 268 Harvard sophomores selected in 1938-42 and followed prospectively for seven decades until 2009. However, before I present the data that underscore the importance of relationships, I need to provide the reader with some background.

Begun in 1938, the study harnessed medical and psychological sciences in order to understand what determines health rather than illness. The study designer was the Student Health Service Director, Arlie Bock. He hoped that the research would help the United States better select officer candidates. So the study was initially interested in identifying leaders and supermen, not best friends.

The study's predictive criteria included: vital affect, athletic prowess, masculine (as contrasted to feminine) body builds, intelligence, perseverance on a treadmill, and friendliness (a variable more correlated with extraversion than capacity for intimacy). These variables were all inter-correlated, and they correlated well with the men's global A, B, C rating—assigned at the end of college to indicate prognosis for future success.

If the importance of relationships had not occurred to any of the originators of the study, neither had the capacity for warm, intimate relationships crossed the minds of social scientists anywhere else. Many psychiatrists believed that personality was determined by body build. Many social scientists still believed that the British Empire had been built on racial superiority, not on the luck of "guns, germs and steel," and that instincts, not relationships, ruled the unconscious. In the 1940's my high school English teacher drilled into us Kipling's mantra, "He travels fastest who travels alone."

We forget how recent is an abiding interest in the importance of close relationships. During ten hours of interviews, the Study men had been queried about masturbation and premarital sex but not about best friends or girlfriends.

With this introduction, let me lay out 70 years of evidence that our relationships with other people matter, and matter more than anything else in the world. I shall examine the power of the childhood and young adult variables to predict rewarding lives from age 50-80.

My criteria for a rewarding late life comprise a decathlon of what we call "events." Two events reflecting economic success were high earned income and high occupational prestige. Four events reflecting biological success were being still alive by age 80 and if so, in good health—both physically and mentally, as well as both subjectively and objectively. Three events reflecting good relationships were a happy marriage (ages 40-70), close father-child relationships, and social support at age 70. The final "event" was early smoking cessation. Sustained smoking, that great destroyer of health, was a marker for alcoholism and major depression—those two great destroyers of relationships.

Although these 10 variables appear disparate, they were highly correlated with each other. So when I use the events related to economic success to make my points below, they are indicative of other outcomes indicating rewarding lives.

There were 8 potential predictors of a rewarding late-life adjustment that were favored by the original investigators. These were relatively independent of close relationships. Two were obvious: IQ and parental social class. Remember, not all these Harvard graduates had been born with silver spoons in their mouths. Half of the students' mothers had not attended college, and fully half of the students needed scholarships and/or worked during the academic year to pay their tuition.

Six other items were theorized by the study to predict good officers and store managers. In only 8 out of a possible 80 matches (8 predictors times 10 outcomes) did any of these variables significantly predict "rewarding" adjustment to life—none of them strongly.

Five common risk variables to successful aging included early ancestral death, alcoholic relatives, depressed relatives, fewer years of education, and childhood developmental problems. These were significant in only 10 out a possible 50 matches.

However, when I, safely ensconced in 21st century science, tested the hypothesis that relationships are the most important prologue to a good life, prediction became far more successful. Since warm relationships are hard enough to measure in the 21st century let alone in 1940, I used four indirect measures.

The first predictor was assessment of a cohesive home-life combined with warm relationships with mother, father, and siblings. This indicator was based on in-depth interviews of both the men and their parents during college and assessed by two independent raters blind to events after 1940. This indicator did not seem important until 1972.

The second predictor was the study staff's A, B, and C consensus rating of the men's overall soundness at age 21.

- **A** = Would have no "serious problem in handling problems that might confront them."
- **B** = "If a boy was lacking in warmth in his touch with people" or too "sensitive."
- **C** = Men who showed "marked mood variations" or were "markedly asocial."

The third predictor was the "maturity" or "immaturity" of the men's involuntary coping style from 20 to 35. Mature coping mechanisms were "suppression" (patience and stoicism), "altruism" (doing for others what you wished had been done for yourself), and "anticipation" (allowing painful emotions to come consciously to mind before the event). Immature coping mechanisms were "fantasy" (imaginary friends), projection (externalizing blame), "hypochondriasis" (complaining and rejecting help) and "acting out" (tantrums). While often soothing the subject, these immature behaviors do not win friends.

The final predictor "Object Relations (age 30-47)" subtracted points for not being married for more than ten years, not having children, being distant from children, having few friends, no contact with family of origin, no clubs, and no games with others. Although not assessed until age 47, this variable was used because it dramatically predicted future occupational success.

Love predicts income and occupational success. The four measures of warm relationships all strongly correlated with each other. More importantly, these four variables were highly predictive of both income and occupational prestige. Out of the 8 (4 predictors times 2 outcomes of income and occupational success) possible matches, all were significant.

For example, the 58 men with the best scores for "Object Relations" were three times more likely to be in Who's Who in America and their maximum income in 1977 dollars was $81,000 a year. In contrast, the 31 men with the worst "Object Relations" received an average maximum salary of $36,000.

The 41 men with the warmest childhoods earned an average of $81,000 a year. The 84 men with poor childhood relationships reported a maximum earned income of $50,000.

The 12 men with the most mature (empathic) coping style reported an annual income of $123,000 a year; the 16 men with the most immature (narcissistic) coping style reported an income of $53,000 a year.

By way of comparison, the contrast in maximum earned income between men whose parents had been in the upper-upper and in the lower-middle social class was only $4,000—an insignificant difference.

These four relationship-reflecting variables also predicted successful health outcomes. Twenty-five out of 32 (4 variables times 8 health outcomes) were significant, and 12 strongly significant.

Adolescent social class, intelligence, treadmill endurance, and constitution meant little to successful aging of the 1940 Harvard graduates. In contrast, capacity for empathic relationships predicted a great deal.

So I go back to my initial point: happiness equals love, full stop.

Five Actions to Build Love and Be Loved

by Tayyab Rashid

1. Arrange a date with your mate that celebrates both of your signature strengths. Discuss ways in which your strengths complimented each other during the date.

2. Express your love creatively, such as through a poem, note, or sketch. Consider taking a photograph of an important place, event or situation that reminds you of your mutual love.

3. Engage in a favorite activity together, such as hiking, going to an amusement park, biking, walking in the park, swimming, camping, or jogging. If you can't think of a mutual favorite activity, pick one to try together.

4. Tape record your parent's earliest recollections and share them with your children. Help your family record their cherished memories in a similar manner.

5. Make a family blessing journal in which everyone writes good things that happen to them daily. One night a week, read aloud some of the best things from the previous seven days.

Sonnet 141 (Poem)

by William Shakespeare

Read aloud to explore the strength of love and be loved.

In faith, I do not love thee with mine eyes,
For they in thee a thousand errors note;
But 'tis my heart that loves what they despise,
Who in despite of view is pleased to dote.
Nor are mine ears with thy tongue's tune delighted,
Nor tender feeling, to base touches prone,
Nor taste, nor smell, desire to be invited
To any sensual feast with thee alone.

But my five wits nor my five senses can
Dissuade one foolish heart from serving thee,
Who leaves unsway'd the likeness of a man,
Thy proud hearts slave and vassal wretch to be.
Only my plague thus far I count my gain,
That she that makes me sin awards me pain.

Love of Learning

"When people have love of learning as a strength, they are cognitively engaged. They typically experience positive feelings in the process of acquiring skills, satisfying curiosity, building on existing knowledge, and/or learning something completely new." They often pursue knowledge and skills in an organized and disciplined way, and they persist even when there may be no immediate benefit from the acquired knowledge or skill. CSV-103, CSV-163

Shared Love of Learning

by Ryan Niemiec

At the International Positive Psychology Association's charter conference in 2009, I had the opportunity to experience pleasure, engagement, and meaning simultaneously when I sat down with 16 of the leading experts, researchers, and practitioners in positive psychology today. During our video interviews, we explored the lines of connection between their work and the VIA Classification of character strengths and virtues. With the opportunity to sit back, review the tapes and reflect, I've begun to see some themes to share with you here.

I asked each leader to share his or her top VIA character strengths. It may not surprise you that love of learning was the most endorsed strength. In fact, 10 of 16 leaders called it a signature strength.

I explain it this way: As a strength of character, love of learning can be distinguished from curiosity in that it involves systematically building up knowledge and wisdom. Research, especially good scientific research, involves just that – systematic studies to gain new knowledge or new ways of understanding existing knowledge. People with the signature strength of love of learning are confident about their ability to learn, enjoy the process of learning, and find that the act of learning is its own intrinsic reward.

Love of learning is a core mechanism by which these great thinkers and researchers connect deeply with life. For example, two positive psychology researchers and authors, Ed Diener and Todd Kashdan, thrive on being in the laboratory crunching data, curious about new discoveries, and eagerly pursuing new knowledge at any opportunity. Both linked this work to feeling focused, relaxed, yet goal-oriented.

As they described their experiences, both noted an alternation between a state of flow (automatic and absorbed experience) and savoring (consciously relishing the experience). These are two processes that foster learning. Indeed Diener and Kashdan both experience a sense of losing track of time merging with a sense of control in which the activity itself is rewarding.

Love of learning combines in a meaningful way with most character strengths, but the most frequent combination among these leaders was love of learning with curiosity. Curiosity acts as the grease for the motor mechanism of love of learning. It keeps the motor functioning at the highest level. Jonathan Haidt, who researches awe, open-mindedness, and gratitude, explained that curiosity combined with love of learning allows him to experience an incredibly engaging role as an explorer. Like an ethnographer immersed in the study of a new culture, he explores territories in politics, morality, and character not traversed by many, if any, social psychology researchers.

Tayyab Rashid, developer of *positive psychotherapy*, identified his top two strengths as love of learning and social intelligence. This merging of an interpersonal strength and a cognitive strength is a meaningful combination for pursuing knowledge of the true identities of clients. Social intelligence provides a way to get there – the ability to succinctly query, name, and understand the feelings and motives of others.

Barbara Fredrickson, leading researcher on positive emotions, has combined signature strengths of love of learning and appreciation of beauty and excellence – which fits closely with the actual research she is interested in. This combination of strengths explains why she does research on positive emotions in that she pursues and gravitates toward learning more about the beauty of positive experiences.

Figure 15: Share a love of learning

Peterson and his colleagues have found that the character strength called love of learning correlates strongly with the engaged life, more strongly than the pleasurable life or the meaningful life, making it a great strength for anyone wanting to deepen his or her sense of flow and connectedness in work, play, and relationships. Considering the endorsement of this character strength by many of positive psychology's leaders, there is strong reason for optimism as we think about the future of the study of human flourishing.

Five Actions to Build Love of Learning

by Tayyab Rashid

1. Visit a new museum every month and write about new things you learned. Bring a friend or family member and listen to their impressions of the trip.

2. Follow an ongoing global event through newspapers, TV or Internet. Observe the differences in reporting between various sources and evaluate each critically.

3. Read aloud with your loved ones. Take turns picking the reading material in order to share your interests with others.

4. Arrange a teach-learn date with a friend, learn a skill, and teach what you are best at. Try to find a friend with very different interests so that you are exposed to something totally new.

5. Travel to new places and blend education with leisure. While you are there, take a tour or visit a local museum to learn more about the local culture and history.

Letters by Abigail Adams (Excerpts)

Read aloud to explore the strength of love of learning.

"Learning is not attained by chance. It must be sought with ardor and attended with diligence. [...]"

"These are the times in which a genius would wish to live. It is not in the still calm of life, or the repose of a pacific station, that great characters are formed. The habits of a vigorous mind are formed in contending with difficulties. Great necessities call out great virtues. When a mind is raised, and animated by scenes that engage the heart, then those qualities which would otherwise lay dormant, wake into life and form the character of the hero and the statesman. [...]"

"I've always felt that a person's intelligence is directly reflected by the number of conflicting points of view he can entertain simultaneously on the same topic."

"If we mean to have Heroes, Statesmen and Philosophers, we should have learned women. The world perhaps would laugh at me, and accuse me of vanity, but you I know have a mind too enlarged and liberal to disregard the Sentiment. If much depends as is allowed upon the early Education of youth and the first principals which are instill'd take the deepest root, great benefit must arise from literary accomplishments in women."

Open-Mindedness

Open-mindedness is also called judgment and critical thinking. "Open-mindedness is the willingness to search actively for evidence against one's favored beliefs, plans, or goals, and to weigh such evidence fairly when it is available." This strength involves being able to see many points of view, being able to weigh them critically, and being able to make wise judgments. "Good judgment is fulfilling, in part because it leads to good decisions and in part because it contributes to a coherent view of the world. [...] Open-mindedness makes the examined life possible." CSV-101, CSV-144

Too Little, Too Much, Just Right

By Sandy Lewis

For shorthand, I'll call this strength open-mindedness, but remember it also includes judgment and critical thinking. When it is used well, people can be extraordinarily adept at problem solving. They make critical decisions clearly and with solid reasoning. They can be excellent leaders who bring objectivity to situations that might otherwise be ambiguous or highly slanted.

Just Right: Let's look first at someone with this character strength high in his VIA profile, using it to his own advantage and to the advantage of others around him. "Grant" was a US born engineer leading a large technical operation in Latin America. He and his Latin born wife were struggling with a decision about whether to relocate their family to the United States. His region was growing, and he was concerned about the impact of a move away from his young team.

When I first met Grant, I was impressed by his keen self-awareness. His business acumen was razor sharp, he was excellent at execution, and he was also open-minded about the communication and emotional needs of his team and family.

When he realized that he needed to create a 3-year-plan for his family, he developed a better relationship with his wife by involving her. He also developed a system of regular meetings that allowed his employees to emotionally connect with him on a schedule that made sense.

He looked at the needs of both his family and his team critically and was able to take considered action. Grant thought through obstacles clearly while maintaining an open mind to the ideas, needs, and interests of others.

Figure 16: Balance interests

People high in this strength often perform well where formal reasoning is needed, for example in designing new product workflows or troubleshooting bug-prone programs. They see challenges as solvable problems, and they are open to new ideas and alternative approaches.

Open-Mindedness Underused: People who underuse this strength may seem narrow or rigid as they make decisions.

"Jose" was a brilliant biochemist. A PhD with 35 years of experience, he was renowned in his field for finding solutions to seemingly impossible technical problems.

However he had difficulty forming effective relationships with colleagues. When open discussions on policies or procedures occurred, Jose would be quick to judge and take a position, even in the face of other good information. This behavior was limiting his growth in the organization. He began to believe that everyone was against him. He often suffered from "confirmation bias," meaning he only considered information that confirmed what he already thought.

Through some self-awareness work, Jose learned to recognize that his behavior was damaging his relationships and his future career. He began to listen to the input of others and gather fresh data before he made a decision. In other words, he started practicing this character strength more fully.

Open-Mindedness Overused: Some people overuse this strength by considering too many options. Often this shows up as overthinking or ruminating. Rumination can lead to depression. "Shikha" had earned good grades in high school, but when she went to college, she failed her freshman year and was diagnosed with depression.

When Shikha completed her VIA assessment, open-mindedness was at the top of her profile. Considering this, she recognized that she tended to overthink in class to the point that she stopped raising her hand. She also handed in projects late because they never seemed good enough. Shikha said it was as if her Judgment had "turned inward" on her, so that she had trouble settling on any point of view.

Shikha also noted that in her freshman year, she had not taken any classes that would be a good outlet to express this strength. Today she is a thriving science and math major. She has learned to direct her open-mindedness outward in a healthy way.

When overthinking occurs, adults may see so many sides to a question that they talk themselves out of speaking up, missing the opportunity to make valuable contributions.

Recognizing Open-mindedness: How can one recognize this strength in self and others? In my many years in leadership development, I have learned to look for strengths when I work with people. I ask exploratory questions such as, "When are you so engaged in work that you forget yourself?", "What makes you happy?", "What annoys you?" "If your life were to turn out exactly as you hoped, what would it look like?" When I hear systematic approaches to thinking or excitement over ideas and structure, I suspect that judgment, critical thinking, and open-mindedness may be high and in good use.

Conversely, when I hear people share a good idea and then turn it into a negative, or I hear an overarching critical voice regarding themselves, their peers, or family, I begin to suspect some overuse. I also note when people overthink and second-guess themselves.

"Lavonda" was a respected leader who had been promoted to a high position in a global finance organization. Despite praise from peers and superiors, she struggled to believe in her ability. She told me, "I believe that I am doing well in this area, but ..." and then the other shoe would drop. This was detrimental to her beliefs about herself and her performance in her new position. She would hold back comments in meetings and be overly deferential with her new peers and superiors. Eventually, Lavonda learned to hear her inner voice more clearly and recognize when she was overly self-critical. She also used her excellent critical thinking skills to create programs and business plans with which to chart the progress of her team. She was able to use her strength more effectively by identifying where, when, and how it needed to be applied.

So, how do people counteract the potential negative consequences of overuse and allow this strength to be used fully?

Helping people identify how they feel while using their top strengths can help them see when they are using their strengths to their advantage. We can also encourage people to use their strengths more frequently and with intention. Using strengths in novel ways has positive effects on long-term happiness. Perhaps this occurs because people become more able to discern when a strength is used in beneficial ways.

It also helps to talk about complementary strengths. While open-mindedness can be a particularly challenging top strength to use "just right," it helps to temper it with other strengths. "Rahul" who had in descending order, open-mindedness, humor, leadership, appreciation of beauty, and love. When he learned to use his appreciation of beauty through a daily nature walk at lunch, his stress level decreased, and he was able to be far more balanced and make better decisions at work. His relationship with his family also improved because he made room to practice his strength of love!

Each strength can be overused or underused. Building self-awareness helps people keep the best side of a strength at the forefront.

Five Actions to Build Open-Mindedness

by Tayyab Rashid

1. Identify the last three actions that you weren't happy with (such as not following through with a goal) and brainstorm better alternative ideas for the future. Consider both actions and omissions.

2. Ask a trusted and wise friend to critically appraise your judgment on your last three significant actions. Promise them that you will listen to their appraisal without getting angry or defensive.

3. Play devil's advocate on an issue that you have strong opinions about. Thinking through an argument for the other side may open your mind to a new perspective, or it may make your original arguments seem more valid.

4. Identify the last three events during which you did not think through your actions. Develop a method, such as counting to ten, to give yourself time to think before you act next time.

5. Mentor someone of a different ethnic or religious background. Remember that the mentor can learn as much from the student as the student can from the mentor.

On Certain Blindness in Human Beings

by William James

Read aloud to explore the strength of open-mindedness.

Some years ago, while journeying in the mountains of North Carolina, I passed by a large number of 'coves,' as they call them there, or heads of small valleys between the hills, which had been newly cleared and planted. The impression on my mind was one of unmitigated squalor. The settler had in every case cut down the more manageable trees, and left their charred stumps standing. The larger trees he had girdled and killed, in order that their foliage should not cast a shade. He had then built a log cabin, plastering its chinks with clay, and had set up a tall zigzag rail fence around the scene of his havoc, to keep the pigs and cattle out. [...]

The forest had been destroyed; and what had 'improved' it out of existence was hideous, a sort of ulcer, without a single element of artificial grace to make up for the loss of Nature's beauty. Ugly, indeed, seemed the life of the squatter, scudding, as the sailors say, under bare poles, beginning again away back where our first ancestors started, and by hardly a single item the better off for all the achievements of the intervening generations.

Talk about going back to nature! I said to myself, oppressed by the dreariness, as I drove by. Talk of a country life for one's old age and for one's children! Never thus, with nothing but the bare ground and one's bare hands to fight the battle! Never, without the best spoils of culture woven in! The beauties and commodities gained by the centuries are sacred. They are our heritage and birthright. No modern person ought to be willing to live a day in such a state of rudimentariness and denudation.

Then I said to the mountaineer who was driving me, "What sort of people are they who have to make these new clearings?" "All of us," he replied. "Why, we ain't happy here, unless we are getting one of these coves under cultivation." I instantly felt that I

135

had been losing the whole inward significance of the situation. Because to me the clearings spoke of naught but denudation, I thought that to those whose sturdy arms and obedient axes had made them, they could tell no other story. But, when they looked on the hideous stumps, what they thought of was personal victory. [...]

I had been as blind to the peculiar ideality of their conditions as they certainly would also have been to the ideality of mine, had they had a peep at my strange indoor academic ways of life at Cambridge.

And now what is the result of all these considerations and quotations? It is negative in one sense, but positive in another. It absolutely forbids us to be forward in pronouncing on the meaninglessness of forms of existence other than our own; and it commands us to tolerate, respect, and indulge those whom we see harmlessly interested and happy in their own ways, however unintelligible these may be to us. Hands off: neither the whole of truth nor the whole of good is revealed to any single observer, although each observer gains a partial superiority of insight from the peculiar position in which he stands. Even prisons and sickrooms have their special revelations. It is enough to ask of each of us that he should be faithful to his own opportunities and make the most of his own blessings, without presuming to regulate the rest of the vast field.

Persistence

Persistence is "finishing what one has started, keeping on despite obstacles, taking care of business, achieving closure, staying on task, getting it off one's desk and out the door..." Persistence means continuing in spite of boredom, frustration, or difficulty. It also means avoiding the temptation to do something easier and perhaps more pleasurable.

Thus persistence is defined as "a voluntary continuation of a goal-directed action in spite of obstacles, difficulties, or discouragement." CSV-202, CSV-229

Got Grit? Start with Mindset

by Emiliya Zhivotovskaya

Human beings are creatures of habit. We look for patterns, routines and shortcuts to maximize the returns on our expended energy. The need for speed also leads to increased desire for immediate gratification. In an age of e-mail, on-line shopping and text messaging, it is easy to get sucked into wanting things to happen quickly, and if they don't, it's easy to give up.

In his famous "Last Lecture," Randy Pausch, the Carnegie Mellon professor who was given three to six months to live, put a picture of a wall on the screen. He said when a wall appears in front of the things you want, the wall is not there to say, "Do not do it." Instead, the wall is asking, "How badly do you want it?" Essentially, he was calling on his audience to develop the ability to pursue a goal with persistence and passion, a quality sometimes called grit.

People with grit tend to persevere and push themselves toward success. Research suggests that people with grit report experiencing more happiness than those who are less gritty, even when controlling for age and education, and earn higher grade point averages than their non-gritty classmates, even those with higher standardized test scores.

Author Jack Canfield said that if your goal is to chop down a tree and every day you go out and take five swings at it, you will eventually knock it down. It makes sense that putting effort and perseverance towards a goal enables you to achieve it. The question is why do so many people fail to persevere?

In our world, there are barriers to developing grit.

Figure 17: Continue in the face of difficulty

Attention is a hot commodity in an era of the World Wide Web, television advertisements, and endless choices. It is easy to get swept away into the world of options, but getting excited about multiple projects makes it difficult to maintain interest and cultivate grit. As a coach, I have worked with many people that want to leap from being at step 2 to step 20 in no time because of their enthusiasm to move on to the next project.

To help people get past this impatience, I ask them to keep lists of things they want to accomplish in the future. Putting a potential project on a list makes it possible to let it go for now because the list holds a reminder. That enables them to focus on their current projects. Then they can find ways to spice up the current project and use more of their strengths. They can dissect big projects into manageable, achievable tasks. Then they can make them more game-like with rules and guidelines.

Another important aspect of grit is effort. Achievement is a product of talent and time spent on a task. Needing to spend time on task is difficult for some people to accept. Dr. Carol Dweck says they have a *fixed mindset*. People with a fixed mindset believe that needing to spend effort is a bad sign. If they have what it takes, if they are smart and talented by nature, then they should not need to spend much effort. This belief decreases their motivation to work hard towards long-term goals.

Interestingly, according to Dweck, simply learning about fixed mindsets changes in people's belief systems. They are more likely to accept a *growth mindset*, the belief that effort, embracing challenges, and seeking out learning opportunities are stronger predictors of success than built-in abilities. This encourages a grittier perspective, leading to greater investment of effort and time.

A few years ago I completed the New York City half-marathon. This was a stretch goal. I had never run more than 4 miles in my life. It took grit to get to the race and even more to complete it. Nevertheless, afterward I felt so proud and the positive emotions were self-reinforcing. It helps me believe that I can do difficult things and that with time and effort, I can increase my capacity to perform.

Five Actions to Build Persistence

by Tayyab Rashid

1. Set five small goals weekly. Break them into practical steps, accomplish them on time, and monitor your progress from week to week.

2. Select a role model who exemplifies perseverance and determine how you can follow her/his footsteps. If this person is alive and someone you know, speak with him or her about this strength.

3. Seed some flowering plants early in the spring and tend them throughout the summer. Appreciate their life cycle and your role as caretaker.

4. Attend a seminar or workshop on time management. Write the key ideas down and review them weekly.

5. Be aware how to cut your losses in tasks that don't require persistence. Apply your energy where it is most productive.

The Seagull (Monologue)

by Anton Chekhov

Read aloud to explore the strength of persistence.

NINA: What do you mean you kissed the ground I walked on? I don't deserve to live. I'm so tired. If only I could rest – I need rest! I'm the seagull – but I'm not really. I'm an actress. Yes. *(She hears Arkadina and Trigorin laughing.)* So he's here, too...well, it doesn't matter. He never believed in theatre, he always laughed at me for my dreams of being famous, and bit by bit I stopped believing, too, and lost heart...there were all the other things to worry about – love, jealousy...and always the worry about the baby. I became trivial and commonplace. My work lost all meaning. On stage I didn't know what to do with my hands or how to stand, I couldn't control my voice...You can't know what it's like when you're up there feeling you're acting so badly. The seagull. No, that's *not* me...you remember how you once shot that seagull? A man happened to come along and see her, and having nothing much to do, destroyed her. Idea for a short story... No, that's not it ... what was I saying? Oh yes, about acting... I'm not like that anymore. I've become a real actress. I love acting, when I'm on stage I feel drunk on the sheer joy of it, and I feel beautiful. While I've been back here I've spent a lot of time walking and thinking – and every day I've felt my spirit getting stronger. What I've realized, Kostya, is that, with us, whether we're writers or actors, what really counts is not dreaming about fame and glory...but stamina: knowing how to keep going despite everything, and having faith in yourself – I've got faith in myself now and that's helped the pain, and when I think to myself, "You're on the stage!' then I'm not afraid of anything life can to do to me.

Perspective

"Perspective refers to the ability to take stock of life in large terms, in ways that make sense to oneself and other. Perspective ... is the coordination of this information and its deliberate use to improve well-being. In a social context, perspective allows the individual to listen to others, to evaluate what they say, and then to offer good (sage) advice."

People with perspective and wisdom address important and difficult questions about the conduct and meaning of life. Others turn to them for advice. CSV-106, CSV-182

Giving Up when You Can't Cut the Mustard

by Dan Tomasulo

I ran out of money the last year of my PhD in psychology and had to get a full-time job. I took a position running an experimental group home to take the lowest functioning people out of Willowbrook, the infamous New York State institution known for its negligence and abuse of residents.

It was overwhelming. I lived in the group home and worked 18 hours a day. Between trying to prevent clients from killing each other, studying for my comprehensives, and planning my dissertation I was getting frazzled. Staff members were quitting on me left and right, the regulations that came with running the home were mind-boggling, and the less than warm welcome from the town left me bedraggled, frustrated, and edgy. I decided to talk to my dissertation advisor and mentor, Dr. Cohen.

Dr. Cohen was the most published of anyone in the university and yet had the reputation of being both kind and wise. His perspective on things often brought guidance through understanding. He could bring clarity out of confusion.

His large and imposing office was the kingdom of the intellect. Floor to ceiling books and journals. He was always busy putting things back on his shelves. When I came to see him, he invited me to have a seat, and he continued shelving books as we talked.

"Hello," I said.

He motioned toward the chair facing his desk in the center of the room. I sat down.

"I'm just so overwhelmed I didn't know what to do. There's just a lot going on," I said, cutting to the chase.

"Like what?"

"I don't know what I'm doing with these profoundly disturbed people. I'm not sleeping, I can't hold on to staff, I've got a nonverbal violent woman with an IQ of 36, a 7 foot tall man with gigantism, a man with pica, synesthesia, and encopresis, a woman with Prader-Willi and with intermittent explosive disorder, a Down Syndrome man who mumbles and I can't understand at all, and a woman who is catatonic."

The professor was lost in rearranging books and didn't answer.

"And my staff? I take a week to interview and hire someone only to have them last 2 days —and I'm distracted."

He was still putting books away.

"Violent woman, giant, pica. Synesthesia, encopresis," he said pausing, "Interesting, Prader-Willi, intermittent explosive, catatonic, Down Syndrome, interesting. No good staff, and you're distracted, yes?"

"Yeah, this is my life, and if I don't get my degree I can't get a university job, or a license. I can't get this all done," I said throwing up my hands. "I'm out of control. I can't take care of everyone and myself. I can't handle the paperwork and bureaucracy. I can't do it all!"

He came over to me and stood alongside. He put his left hand on my right shoulder and took a deep breath.

"Give up."

"What?"

"I recommend you give up."

He patted me on the shoulder twice, and then went back to his books.

"Give up?"

"Yes, of course. Nothing is working out how you planned, your personal life is chaotic, and you're overwhelmed with responsibilities, and have no idea what is going to happen, yes?"

"That's true."

"So give up."

"What about my dissertation?"

The professor waved his hand dismissively. "Let it go. What do you need that for? All it is going to do is prepare you for a career with disturbed people, more headaches, disappointments, and obstacles. I say let it go," he said as he continued going through boxes on the floor.

"Just like that?"

"Just like that."

"Just give up?"

"Just give up," he said, studying one of the books. "Just give up and do nothing. Maybe get a hotdog pushcart in the city. Sell hot dogs on the street. It is a good living, you are your own boss, and you are independent. I see you as a hot dog vendor."

"You think I should sell hot dogs?"

"Yes, the good ones."

I didn't know what to say.

"Of course you will have to get a permit to have a business, a pushcart business, from the city," he said casually, "and insurance, for when someone sues you because the hot dogs were not cooked well enough."

I nodded.

"And you will need to display a certificate of inspection approval from the Board of Health. They are picky and difficult, but you can deal with them."

I couldn't believe what I was hearing.

"And, people will criticize you and your good hot dogs. And hoodlums will steal your fine food, and try to rob you at night when you come home with cash."

Figure 18: Open a hot dog stand

I nodded like I was one of those dolls with the bobbing head in the back of a car.

"You will be frightened about walking home, but you can hire bodyguards. And be sure to get up early so no one steals your good spot on the street. Are you a good fist-fighter?"

Finally, I understood.

"Thank you," I said. He continued to put his books away.

"Yes. I recommend you give up, and prepare for a life of ease."

Dr. Cohen's perspective helped me recommit to my goals and work more efficiently and effectively. Within the year I finished my dissertation, got a job teaching, and eventually got my license. By showing me that no job is easy he helped me get back on track.

Perspective is one of the powerhouses inside the virtue of wisdom. It is more than just high intelligence in that it involves taking in views from all sides before rendering a decision. Research shows that perspective is in the top 10 strengths used at work, highly valued by high school students, central to the engagement route to happiness, a good predictor of a student's GPA, and an important defense against the negative effects of stress and trauma.

I'm now in the position to counsel graduate students. They make appointments with me when they are confused, overwhelmed, or directionless. I suppose they believe I have perspective. My advice? "Have you ever thought about selling hot dogs: The good ones?"

Five Actions to Build Perspective

by Tayyab Rashid

1. Find purpose in the last five of your significant actions/decisions. Recall what motivated you to make the decisions that you made.

2. Find someone wise (either someone still alive or someone who has passed on), read or watch a film on his or her life, and identify how their life can guide your decisions and actions. Consider the philosophy that the person followed and compare it to your own.

3. Offer advice, but only when asked and only after listening empathically to the seeker. Ask for advice from that person in return in the near future.

4. Build a network of friends and confidants with differing perspectives. Seek their council when you need expertise and offer your own perspective should they ask for it.

5. Mentor a child in your neighborhood. Remember a role model that you had as a child and try to emulate their qualities.

Gettysburg Address (Speech)

By Abraham Lincoln

November 19, 1863

Read aloud to explore the strength of perspective.

Four score and seven years ago our fathers brought forth on this continent, a new nation, conceived in Liberty, and dedicated to the proposition that all men are created equal.

Now we are engaged in a great civil war, testing whether that nation, or any nation so conceived and so dedicated, can long endure. We are met on a great battle-field of that war. We have come to dedicate a portion of that field, as a final resting place for those who here gave their lives that that nation might live. It is altogether fitting and proper that we should do this.

But, in a larger sense, we cannot dedicate -- we cannot consecrate -- we cannot hallow -- this ground. The brave men, living and dead, who struggled here, have consecrated it, far above our poor power to add or detract. The world will little note, nor long remember what we say here, but it can never forget what they did here. It is for us the living, rather, to be dedicated here to the unfinished work, which they who fought here have thus far so nobly advanced. It is rather for us to be here dedicated to the great task remaining before us -- that from these honored dead we take increased devotion to that cause for which they gave the last full measure of devotion -- that we here highly resolve that these dead shall not have died in vain -- that this nation, under God, shall have a new birth of freedom -- and that government of the people, by the people, for the people, shall not perish from the earth.

Prudence

"Prudence is a cognitive orientation to the personal future, a form of practical reasoning and self-management that helps to achieve the individual's long-term goals effectively. Prudent individuals show a farsighted and deliberative concern for the consequences of their actions and decisions, successfully resist impulses, ... have a flexible and moderate approach to life, and strive for balance among their goals and ends." CSV-478

In Praise of Prudence

by Kathryn Britton

During an energy crisis many years ago, when we were all worried about gas supplies and tired of waiting in lines at the gas pumps, I read an article in my company's newsletter about ways to save fuel. One suggestion was to take the spare tire out of the trunk of the car. The author argued that you almost never need it, and its weight adds to gas consumption for every use of the vehicle.

Needless to say, I didn't rush to take the spare tire out of my car. True, I'd been lucky never to need it yet, but I could imagine finding myself by the side of the road with a flat tire. I could imagine how sorry I'd be if there weren't a spare available. I was willing to pay a small price with every car trip to be prepared for the one that went wrong. This is the same thinking that prompts me to pay high premiums for health insurance while still entertaining the strong hope that I won't need to use it.

That ability to project forward, to imagine possible outcomes, and to make sensible judgments, is a quality of the character strength called prudence, caution, and discretion.

This is an under-appreciated strength. Imagine for a moment a group of people that has taken the VIA assessment of character strengths and then gathered to share top strengths. Most will speak up gladly and confidently with "Social Intelligence," "Curiosity," "Bravery," "Creativity," "Spirituality," and so on. But for those whose top strength is "Humility" or "Prudence," what would you expect?

Figure 19: Glad to have the spare tire in the trunk

Years ago, I read a report about focus groups conducted with high school students to explore their understanding of the VIA strengths. Generally speaking, adolescents understood them quite well, but I remember they had a tendency to confuse humility with humiliation and prudence with prudes. Caution and prudence seemed kind of stuffy and timid. Maybe adults are a little more discriminating with language, but still people seem a bit disappointed to find prudence on the top of their lists. Is this because people nowadays tend to glorify risk-taking? Is it because they don't fully appreciate the value of prudence to a well-lived life?

Let's think about what prudence entails. It involves thinking ahead to discern what leads to good outcomes and what does not. Think about all that entails: being able to project today's actions into the future, to imagine the possible outcomes, and to form judgments about alternatives. I expect a person with the character strength prudence must have a high tolerance for ambiguity, needing to deal with incomplete and often conflicting information in order to make judgments.

Psychologist Nick Haslam identifies the following qualities of prudence:

1. A foresighted stance toward the future, holding long-term goals and aspirations in mind
2. Ability to resist self-defeating impulses and to persist in beneficial activities, even if they lack immediate appeal (Grit anyone?)
3. Reflective, deliberate, and practical thinking about life choices
4. Ability to harmonize multiple goals that may initially conflict

    Imagine getting a job offer in a distant city. The job is very exciting, but it requires you to move your family. Your spouse already has a good job and isn't eager to change. Your children don't want to change schools. The new job will be closer to your spouse's family but further from your family. Now you have to harmonize your goals of career advancement and family well-being.

5. Ability to seek personal good without being destructive with respect to the needs of people around you

So prudence is much more than carrying a spare tire in the car. It involves imagining the future. It involves creating, assessing, and harmonizing multiple goals. It may involve making hard choices.

Prudence involves the ability to picture the future. For many, this may mean being able to picture a better future and to plan actions that bring that future about. Fred Soper was a pioneer epidemiologist working toward a world without all the human suffering that comes from malaria. His behavior demonstrates that prudence does not have to involve playing it safe or settling for small goals. Prudence involves practical judgment, not unthinking optimism. Soper's plans were pragmatic, based on observation and fieldwork. He addressed the threat of malaria from multiple viewpoints. He didn't try to solve it in just one way. So he probably set multiple goals and had to bring them together in his one life.

Picture a world where people think about the long-term implications of their actions. See them thinking about their carbon footprints when they make major life decisions, such as where to live and work, or everyday decisions such as where to shop and play.

There's a French saying that only a family will plant an oak avenue because it takes so long to grow. To make that much effort, you have to picture your grandchildren walking along under the leafy trees. Certainly there's a lot of short-term thinking going on today, with companies that look only at next quarter's profits, with politicians that focus on short-term gains. But perhaps if we spoke with admiration for the long-term thinking of prudence, we'd see people taking actions that benefit the entire family of life.

Viva Prudence!

Five Actions to Build Prudence

by Tayyab Rashid

1. Think twice before saying anything. Do this exercise at least ten times a week and note its effects.

2. Drive cautiously and note that there are fewer time-bound emergencies than you actually think. Make highway safety a priority, especially at busy times such as rush hour and holiday weekends.

3. Remove all extraneous distractions before your make your next three important decisions. Take the time to clear your mind and gather your thoughts.

4. Visualize the consequences of your decisions in one, five, and ten years' time. Take these long-term consequences into account when making short-term choices.

5. Make important decisions when you are relaxed, rather than when you are anxious or depressed. If you must make a decision under pressure, take a few seconds to breathe deeply and clear your mind.

We May be Brothers After All (Speech)

by Chief Sealth

Read aloud to explore the strength of prudence.

The Great Chief in Washington sends word that you wish to buy our land. The idea of selling land is strange to us, but we will consider your offer.

How can you buy or sell the sky, the warmth of the land? If we do not own the air and the sparkle of the water, how can you buy them? We are part of the earth and it is part of us.

The mountains, the meadows, the deer, the great eagle, and man – all belong to the same family. This will not be easy. The land is sacred to us. The rivers are our brothers, and yours, and you must give the rivers the kindness you would give any brother.

If we accept, I will make one condition. The white man must treat the beasts of this land as his brothers. If all the beasts are gone, man would die from loneliness of spirit. All things are connected.

The air is precious to us. The air shares its spirit with all like and if we sell you our land you must keep it sacred as a place that even the white man can go to taste the wind and smell the meadow's flowers.

Everything is connected. We may be brothers; we shall see. One thing we know; our God is the same as yours.

The earth is precious to Him. Even the white man cannot be exempt from the common destiny. We may be brothers.

We shall see.

Chief Sealth is also known as Chief Seattle. The city of Seattle was named after him.

Self-Regulation

"Self-regulation refers to how a person exerts control over his or her own responses so as to pursue goals and live up to standards." Often this involves overriding an initial impulse or being able to redirect thought away from an undesirable behavior. Sometimes it involves being able to initiate behaviors, such as getting out of bed to get to work on time. CSV-500

This is Your Brain on Habits

by Emily vanSonnenberg

How many of you admit to having at least one bad habit you'd rather do without? If you're honest with yourself–that is, if you realize that you're human–then you nodded your head. Pick your head up, because there is good news: habits are learned. Therefore, you can unlearn bad habits and learn new habits to replace those undesirable ones!

How? Let's explore the brain's mechanisms that underlie habit formation and what it takes to form new habits.

A habit is automatic behavior that occurs without much conscious thought.

Habit is often thought of as the automatic behavioral engagement in a destructive activity. However often that is true, a habit can also be automatic behavioral engagement in an activity that promotes well-being. Would you like to possess new and positive habits that do, in fact, serve you well?

Perhaps the thoughts that now come to mind are, "Awww geez, how much effort will I have to expend to get into the positive habit of exercising every day before work (or writing in a gratitude journal every night before bed or devoting more energy to my friendships or drinking more water or eating my vegetables)?"

It will, undoubtedly, require effort to form new and positive habits. Enter self-regulation. With concerted, disciplined effort over a period of time, frequently repeated behaviors can become automatic. By using some of the willpower lurking within you, new positive behaviors can become habits.

Some researchers have identified areas located within the brain that account for habit formation, namely the basal ganglia, which play a large role in movement control, emotion, cognition, and reward-based learning. Within the basal ganglia, there are two areas responsible for the functions that work in unison to form habits. One part controls movement and is connected to sensorimotor functioning (seeing, hearing, moving, and so on), while the other controls flexible behavior and is connected to areas where associations are recognized and formed.

For example, when we move a part of our body in a new way and it feels good, like salsa dancing, these parts of the brain are active. That's where associations are made when we feel a sense of accomplishment for having tried something new. Our brain then experiences that this new activity is one that serves us well.

Okay, so you tried something once. How long must the new behavior be repeated until the behavior becomes a habit?

There is no one standard time period for a habit to form. It can take anywhere from two weeks to eight months. It depends on the difficulty of the activity being learned and the individual's level of commitment.

For example, it is markedly easier to form the habit to drink one glass of water every day than it is to do 60 sit-ups every morning before work. Studies have shown that on average, participants learning to form a new habit succeeded within 66 days. By the 66-day mark, activities had hit their plateau of learning increases, and thus, the behaviors had become as automatic as they would ever become.

There is an important caveat to keep in mind regarding learning a new habit: early practice of the activity results in greater increases in automaticity. So, if you're going to miss a day from your repeated daily practice of learning a new habit, skip a day that is further along in the 66-day period, since the increase in learning is greatest at the onset.

Figure 20: Drink more water

If you want to break a bad habit, here is one method that is often successful:

- Identify the negative habit you want to break.
- Select a positive habit to adopt in its place.
- Identify the new behavior you will perform to begin forming the positive habit. See below for examples.
- Recognize the sensory impulse(s) in your body that occur just before you usually carry out the negative habit.
- Whenever the impulse occurs, instead of acting habitually, use your conscious attention to perform the new and positive behavior.

Continue practicing the substitution for at least 66 days. You are using the triggers from the old habit to stimulate reinforcement of the new habit.

Here are a few ideas for new positive behaviors that you could substitute for habits you want to extinguish. These behaviors could enhance your well-being by increasing positive emotions, meaning, close relationships, and accomplishment. To increase the likelihood that the new habit will stick, select a behavior that fits your personality and lifestyle.

- Keep a gratitude journal at night. Reach for it when you find yourself wanting to complain about your boss.

- When you find yourself wanting to reach for a drink beyond your limit, play a game like Tetris or Sudoku. The game can give you similar neurochemical rewards.

- If it is hard to get motivated to exercise, try working out with a buddy. This can increase accountability and build relationships. Try exercising in the morning since people are better able to self-regulate earlier in the day.

- Create an 'If-then' intention to implement whenever you want to go to the refrigerator for an extra snack. For example: *If I want an extra snack, then I will do 10 pushups and drink a glass of water first.*

Acquiring a new habit tends to take just over two months until it becomes an automatic response. Use the willpower inside yourself to commit to repeating the behavior. Soon you will no longer need to think about doing the positive behavior. It will become automatic. Don't worry if self-regulating your behaviors depletes your energy, because it might. According to research, one quick and easy way to replenish your ability to self-regulate when exhausted is by watching something that makes you laugh!

You can develop good habits or bad habits. Take your pick. If you consciously behave the way you want to behave for only a few months, it grows markedly easier. Positive habits can have life-changing effects. It is within your control to build them.

"We are what we repeatedly do; excellence then is not an act, but a habit." ~Aristotle

Five Actions to Build Self-Regulation

by Tayyab Rashid

1. Monitor and eliminate distractions such as phone, TV, and Internet while focusing on a particular assignment. Allow yourself short breaks to avoid burnout.

2. Eliminate objects of temptation: when dieting, don't keep junk food around; when abstaining from alcohol, don't socialize in bars; when quitting smoking, replace cigarettes with chewing gum; when cutting back on shopping, leave credit cards or money at home. Ask others that you interact with to respect the removal of tempting items and to encourage your positive lifestyle changes.

3. Next time you get upset, try to control your emotions and focus on positive attributes of the situation. Become aware of the degree to which you can control your feelings and reactions.

4. Carefully create routines that you can follow through systematically. Make minor adjustments as needed but keep the core elements intact.

5. Pay close attention to your biological clock. Do your most important tasks when you are most alert.

Othello (Monologue)

by William Shakespeare

Read aloud to explore the strength of self-regulation.

Iago: Virtue? A fig! 'Tis in ourselves that we are thus
or thus. Our bodies are our gardens, to the which our
wills are gardeners. So that if we will plant nettles
or sow lettuce, set hyssop and weed up thyme, supply
it with one gender of herbs or distract it with many
either to have it sterile with idleness, or manured with industry—
why, the power and corrigible authority of
this lies in our wills. If the balance of our lives had not
one scale of reason to poise another of sensuality, the
blood and baseness of our natures would conduct us
to most prepost'rous conclusions. But we have
reason to cool our raging motions, our carnal
stings, our unbitted lusts. Whereof I take this that
you call love to be a sect or scion.

Social Intelligence

Social intelligence involves insights into one's own motivations and the motivations of others. It is relevant for interpersonal relationships, and it has a moral flavor.

Social intelligence is a form of intelligence because it emphasizes the ability to understand similarities and differences among things and to recognize patterns. "Social intelligence concerns one's relationships with people, including the social relationships involved in intimacy and trust, persuasion, group memberships, and political power." CSV-299, CSV-338-339

Empathy and What it Teaches Us

by Aren Cohen

Christopher Peterson said that positive psychology could be summed up in 3 words: "Other people matter." What is it that makes other people matter to us? Empathy.

Empathy is commonly defined as the ability to understand and share the feelings of another. Being able to relate to another person creates the context in which they have meaning to us. If we cannot understand another person, why should they matter to us? By having insight into how another person feels, we can participate in her experience and comprehend the emotions, good, bad or indifferent, that she feels. Empathy makes us better people because it takes us outside of ourselves. It forces us to acknowledge people around us as human, replete with the same panoply of feelings that we ourselves possess. Empathy allows us to appreciate others because we partake in their emotional lives.

A few years ago, I attended The Wonderplay Conference: Early Childhood Learning in New York City. The theme of the conference was Building Empathy and Resilience: The Role of the Early Educator. The conference was a full day affair with two keynote speakers in the morning and two breakout sessions in the afternoon. While all of the content was fascinating, the presentation I found most stimulating was Dr. Kyle Pruett's "Empathy and the Teachable Moment."

Dr. Pruett's definition of empathy is "mindful perception of another's emotional experience." He discussed how empathy is more powerful than sympathy (defined as emotional resonance) or self-awareness (which would be akin to projecting our own feelings on others or anthropomorphizing animals). Unlike the other two, empathy engenders a sense of reciprocal obligation in us. When we are sympathetic, we care, up to a point. When we are empathic, we feel what another feels, and we are moved to act on his or her behalf. We jump up and down with her if she's joyful; we enfold him in a bear hug if he is sad.

Where does empathy come from? How does it develop within us as children, so that we become empathic adults? Child psychologists Anna Freud and Jean Piaget believed that empathy was part of our moral development. Children learning empathy signifies that they have learned that the world is not "all about me."

Dr. Pruett walked his audience through the *empathic trajectory*, which described how children's brains develop empathy from ages 0-8. At 9 months children learn that others have emotions. Between a year and 18 months, a child will reach out and loan her binky or blanket to an unhappy friend. As children get older, they develop sympathetic and helping behaviors, and then they learn to move beyond themselves, as their brains mature and their use of language grows. By the time children are 7 or 8, they have moved beyond the basic idea of "what is fair," to start creating their own ideas of moral reasoning and social justice.

Dr. Pruett raised questions about how we teach empathy, or if it is programmed in us by nature. Additionally, he asked the audience if we believe there is a difference in the way the two genders exhibit empathy. While fascinating conversations came out of these queries, it seems that much more research is needed.

Figure 21: Offer comfort

Social intelligence is the act of mindful perception of another's emotional experience. We know that other people matter, but the *way* they matter to us is deeply important. Without empathy, people are, in a way, just placeholders. Empathy makes us respond to the feelings of other people.

It was meaningful to me that early educators are exploring how, or if, empathy is teachable. When I think about all the good positive interventions we know, I realize there are few that exercise our empathy.

In their book, *Why Good Things Happen to Good People*, Dr. Stephen Post and Jill Neimark discuss the many benefits of giving. They define giving broadly, not just in the material sense, but also other ways of giving one's self, including celebration, loyalty, humor, and respect. What strikes me about this kind of

163

giving is that it is only possible with empathy. Giving benefits us because it allows us to make others feel good. We understand that we have done this through our own empathy. It is, in fact, the golden rule we learn at age 7 or 8, "Do unto others as you would have them do unto you." What is unexpected is that doing unto others is positive for us. Using our empathy to give provides us with psychological and physical rewards.

When times are hard, we increase the happiness in the world most when we to reach out to others and are generous with them, not just with things, but with spirit and soul.

Five Actions to Build Social Intelligence

by Tayyab Rashid

1. Listen to your friends and siblings empathically, without preparing rebuttals, and simply reflect your feelings after they are finished. Don't just wait for your turn to speak during conversation.

2. If someone offends you, attempt to find at least one positive element in his or her motives. Consider reasons why their offensive behavior may result from temporary, situational factors rather than from their disposition or nature.

3. Write five personal feelings daily for four weeks and monitor patterns. Are there situations that you encounter regularly that alter your emotional pattern?

4. Ask someone close to you about times you did not emotionally understand him/her and how he/she would like to be emotionally understood in the future. Think of a few small, practical steps that you can take when interacting with this person next.

5. Identify which of your friends relate most empathically with others. Observe them closely and try to emulate the social skills that you admire in them.

How I Learned to Drive (Monologue)

by Paula Vogel

Read aloud to explore the strength of social intelligence.

Female Greek Chorus: (As Aunt Mary.) My husband was such a good man – is. Is such a good man. Every night, he does the dishes. The second he comes home, he's taking out the garbage, or doing yard work, lifting the heavy things I can't. Everyone in the neighborhood borrows Peck – it's true – women with husbands of their own, men who just don't have Peck's abilities – there's always a knock on our door for a jump start on cold mornings, when anyone needs a ride, or help shoveling the sidewalk - I look out, and there Peck is, without a coat, pitching in.

I know I'm lucky. The man works from dawn to dusk. And the overtime he does every year – my poor sister. She sits every Christmas when I come to dinner with a new stole, or diamonds, or with the tickets to Bermuda.

I know he has troubles. And we don't talk about them. I wonder, sometimes, what happened to him during the war. The men who fought World War II didn't have "rap sessions" to talk about their feelings. Men in his generation were expected to be quiet about it and get on with their lives. And sometimes I can feel him just fighting the trouble – whatever has burrowed deeper than the scar tissue – and we don't talk about it. I know he's having a bad spell because he comes looking for me in the house, and just hangs around me until it passes. And I keep my banter light – I discuss a new recipe, or sales, or gossip – because I think domesticity can be a balm for men when they're lost. We sit in the house and listen to the peace of the clock ticking in his well-ordered living room, until it passes.

166

Spirituality

Spirituality is also labeled religiousness, faith, and purpose. People with this character strength "have coherent beliefs about the higher purpose and meaning of the universe and [their] place within it." For the vast majority of people, "religiousness and spirituality comfortably coexist. For other people, though, we need to allow for the possibility that they can have a coherent belief system about the transcendent aspects of life that is forged and followed outside traditional religions." CSV-533

Exercise for Spiritual Fitness

By Diana Boufford

How do people build spiritual fitness even as they experience the physical, social, financial, cognitive, and memory losses that occur throughout life, but more frequently and rapidly in old age?

Sometimes due to illness or life circumstances, symptoms of earlier stress reactions come back in older people. Mrs. M, an 89-year-old woman, was a survivor of the Siberian death camps of World War II. When she had to come into transitional care, she found herself lapsing into depression as flashbacks of her years in the death camp resurfaced.

When I went to see her, she told me that due to the chronic pain recovering from surgery and to the necessity of being away from home among strangers, she found herself feeling frightened, lonely, and worried, much like she had felt when her family was forced onto the cattle cars that transported them to the camps. She was desperate to return home to her husband, who needed her to care for him, but her own recovery was slow, keeping her in the rehabilitation facility.

I shared with Mrs. M the story of Viktor Frankl who had been at Auschwitz at the same time that she was in Siberia. From his witnessing and suffering, a belief emerged that people are able to survive nearly anything when they have a purpose and meaning for their survival.

Then I asked Mrs. M, "What was it that you were able to do, that you survived Siberia when so many did not?"

Figure 22: What helped me survive? Compassion

She reflected upon this for a few moments. She then looked at me and said "Compassion. It was compassion that let me survive that horrible place."

"How was that?" I asked.

She then explained to me that there was another young girl there (Mrs. M was 14 when taken prisoner) who was intensely agitated because she was so terribly infested with lice. She had horrible sores on her head, and the blood would run down her face from the wounds created from her scratching and the biting of the bugs.

"I told her," said Mrs. M, "that the only way to help this is to brush your hair every day! I taught her how to care for her hair.

That was all I could do. I think it was the compassion I felt for her, and for everyone else, that helped me survive."

I suggested to Mrs. M that she could draw upon these same feelings and skills to help her cope with being away from home and the pain and work of recovery. She agreed. Within two weeks, she went home. Before she left the nursing home, staff reported that her coping had improved, as had her mood. She was observed engaging in conversations with others more often, and assisting some of the other residents in their daily routines.

This story beautifully illustrates the idea of post-traumatic growth, where some people, despite trauma and suffering, recover and even surpass their levels of previous functioning by growing in other areas of their lives.

I believe that one of the cornerstones for the development of Spiritual Fitness is the ability to move beyond one's basic needs and wants to serve something greater than oneself. Spiritual growth can occur during periods of trauma and hardship. People need a sense of purpose and meaning in life to sustain them. When this meaning is reignited, quality of life can be significantly improved. Even people who are unable to do much anymore can serve by accepting gracefully the service of others, recognizing that their needs give others purpose and meaning.

For those who are grieving serious losses or adversity I often employ another concept in Dr. Frankl's work:

Despair equals suffering without meaning.

When people can find some meaning in their suffering, they can avoid falling into despair, and they can find strength and resolve to overcome the suffering. When people feel there is no meaning, they succumb to despair and hopelessness.

Often elders spend much time and attention reviewing their lives. They contemplate the choices they made, both what worked and what did not. They often appear to review the challenges in their lives systematically, attempting resolution.

Those who are able to reflect upon their lives and come to accept themselves and the various choices they made with compassion and forgiveness will often move forward toward feeling at peace with themselves and others.

They can be fairly happy with themselves and feel that their lives were well-lived, despite the mistakes. Often they will say that the mistakes yielded great learning leading to a greater good.

Those who fail to make this journey or who do not come to forgive themselves will often fall into despair. They may become weighed down with sadness or bitterness, feeling that it is too late and too much damage has been done. Often they find themselves in an endless loop of remembering and condemning themselves or others, further escalating the suffering. They see no meaning in the suffering, but they continue to wallow in it. Couple this with multiple losses which occur more frequently in the elder years, and you have people that require treatment for a major depressive disorder and may be at risk of suicide.

By contrast, people can find their days imbued with meaning and purpose achieved through life reviews that focus on resolution, forgiveness, and celebration. Reminiscence can occur in group settings or pairings, in which memories are shared through storytelling, mentoring, and friendships. Losses, the death of family, friends, and fellow residents, even their own mortality can be made more meaningful through sharing their insights and wisdom.

Through sharing, people are supported as they move through their grief journeys. Growing one's spirit and then ensuring that the wisdom gleaned throughout a lifetime is passed on is among life's most powerful and spiritually enlightened activities. Dare I say, it is a moral, ethical, and spiritual responsibility that anyone can achieve.

People can find great spiritual growth and contentment even in the winter of their lives with appropriate tools and support.

Here are some activities that can help people exercise for spiritual fitness:

Gratitude Letter: Write a letter to someone who made a difference in your life whom you never properly thanked. Letters may even be to people who are already dead.

Three good things: Keep a journal and record daily three good things that occurred and why they were meaningful to you.

Life review: Allow yourself to revisit the more difficult times in your life. Explore all the skills and insights that you developed as a result of the challenges. What good came of these? What did you learn? Were you able to pass this learning on to others? How has your learning served you and others?

Reminiscence Groups: Participate in reminiscence groups sharing the various joys and hardships in your life. Listen attentively to the stories of others. Further your capacity for compassion and acceptance.

Grieving: All losses involve grief. Be willing to cry, honor, and let go a little bit each day. Don't hold on to the sadness and loss. Embrace and nurture the love and memories instead. Be a witness and companion to someone else who is grieving.

Mentoring: Mentor someone, or allow someone to mentor you. Remember it is an act of generosity to receive.

Serving: Do things that benefit others. Be a good listener, offer a warm touch, and recognize the humanity of the people that serve you.

Forgiveness: Forgive yourself and others. Be willing to let go of old grudges and live with greater love and freedom. "Holding on to resentments is like taking poison and waiting for the other person to die," (author unknown).

Prayer and meditation: I have often heard that prayer is speaking with God, and meditation is listening. Taking time to quiet your mind and connect with your innermost self grows your capacity to live in a peaceful, grounded, and loving place.

Using some of these exercises to reflect, share, and forgive, even people with great physical and mental limitations can find meaning in the suffering that comes from the multiple losses of life.

Five Actions to Build Spirituality

by Tayyab Rashid

1. Spend ten minutes daily in breathing deeply, relaxing, and meditating (emptying the mind of thoughts by focusing on breathing). Observe how you feel afterward.

2. Read a spiritual or religious book every day for half an hour. Discuss the ideas in it with someone you trust and respect.

3. Explore different religions – take a class, research over the Internet, meet a person of different religion, or attend the congregation of a different religion. Speak to people who practice this faith and get to know them as people.

4. Explore a fundamental purpose of your life and link your actions to it. Each day, ask yourself if you accomplished anything toward fulfilling this purpose.

5. Write your eulogy or ask your loved ones how they would like to remember you. Do they mention your signature strengths?

A Raisin in the Sun (Monologue)

by Lorraine Hansberry

Read aloud to explore the strength of spirituality.

Beneatha: When I was small... we used to take our sleds out in the wintertime and the only hills we had were the ice-covered stone steps of some houses down the street. And we used to fill them in with snow and make them smooth and slide down them all day...and it was very dangerous, you know... far too steep... and sure enough one day a kid named Rufus came down too fast and hit the sidewalk and we saw his face just split open right there in front of us... And I remember standing there looking at his bloody open face thinking that was the end of Rufus. But the ambulance came and they took him to the hospital and they fixed the broken bones and sewed it all up... and the next time I saw Rufus he just had a little line down the middle of his face.... I never got over that... What one person could do for another, fix him up – sew up the problem, make him all right again. That was the most marvelous thing in the world... I wanted to do that.

I always thought it was the one concrete thing in the world a human being could do. Fix up the sick, you know – and make them whole again. This was truly being God.

Teamwork

The character strength teamwork is also called citizenship, social responsibility, and loyalty. An individual with this strength, "has a strong sense of duty, works for the good of the group rather than for personal gain, is loyal to friends, and can be trusted to pull his or her weight."

"They do this not because external circumstances force them but because they regard it as what a group member should do." CSV-357, CSV-370

Teamwork Levels the Status Playing Field

by Shannon Polly

It was dark in the theater. The crowd was hushed waiting for the big reveal. The musical was *Sweeney Todd*, and my college audience had heard from their friends about what happens when the first victim gets the ax (or in this case, the razor). The seat and foot on the trick chair drop, and the actor falls through the roof of the second floor set to the crash pad below.

At the time, I was backstage waiting for my entrance as Mrs. Lovett. I heard the moment in the music, and then I heard screams. Just like we rehearsed.

But these weren't the screams of an actor playing a character who was just killed. These were real screams. The chair had failed, and the actor was bloodied. It was chaos. There was fog on the stage so no one could really see what was going on, the orchestra didn't know what had happened so they kept playing, and the actor who had bloodied shins and a possibly broken nose was trying to live by the "show must go on" rule. He kept singing and moving to his next entrance.

The other actors, technicians, and musicians knew this was the one exception to the rule. The stage manager stopped the show and went into action. Everyone involved with the

175

production went on high alert. It was a wonderful example of teamwork as a group strength and also teamwork as an individual strength. Each person abandoned his or her ego for what the production needed at that moment. The tech people filled in for each other's duties while the actor was taken to the hospital. The orchestra was waiting poised for their instructions. Even a doctor in the audience offered to come backstage to give medical help. Within 20 minutes the chair was working again and elicited uproarious applause.

If you've ever been in an artistic production you know that there can be many egos involved. But you also know that the best experiences for both actor and audience occur when people set status aside and do what must be done for the good of the production.

Figure 23: Geese fly together

It is possible to overdo teamwork. I was at an impasse coaching a client who described a crushing workload. She worked nights and weekends, balancing being a new manager, her previous work duties, and going back to graduate school. We spent a few sessions probing her values and discussing the benefit of self-care. The light bulb went on for her when we looked at her VIA character strengths and realized that teamwork was a top strength. She put doing her share above her own well-being. After she could see her strength clearly and the signs of overuse, she was able to adjust her behavior to avoid burnout. In the process, she learned to see that delegating work actually served her team, giving others opportunities to grow.

So how do you spot someone with a top strength of teamwork? Watch for the person who identifies with team goals and sometimes puts them ahead of personal gratification, just as my client did. Teamwork involves being able to see the big picture as well as one's place in it.

Here are four ways to build teamwork in oneself and enhance the teams in which you participate.

Approach 1: Place "We" Before "Me": Performance of a Lifetime is an organization in New York City that uses improv to teach the skills of listening, teamwork, and collaboration. In one of their exercises, each person picks two people in the room, one her protector, one her predator. Then they try to place their protectors between them and their predators. What results is usually a flurry of running around the room, people bumping into one another and furiously trying to save themselves from this imaginary threat.

Then the facilitator stops the group and asks the participants to start again and pay attention to how the group is doing. On a second try, all of a sudden, the movement slows down and finally comes to a stop when people take into account the rest of the group and ultimately achieve their goal.

If we are paying attention to how the group is doing, we are letting go of ego, disregarding status and building a better team.

During your next team meeting take a Director Moment. Stop and view the meeting from the balcony and ask yourself, "How is the group doing?" You might ask the team directly to disregard rank or position and ask them to comment on what they see going on in the room.

Approach 2: Invoke Connections to the Group: Remind people that thinking about group membership best serves the whole team. In a research study, two groups of airline flight attendants received different instructions, one focusing on social identity and the other on personal identity. The social identity set prompted people in that group to see themselves as employees of the airline. The personal identity set prompted people to focus on their own experiences and feelings. Both groups read a brief outline of an in-flight event before completing a teamwork questionnaire. People who received the social identity instructions showed greater willingness to engage in coordinated team action with other groups. The status differences between flight attendants and pilots became less salient for them. Each person individually became focused on a larger definition of 'we,' enhancing the strength of teamwork in the group.

Approach 3: Be Open-Minded and Curious: Take an open and curious stance towards the points of view of other team members. Becoming more curious about other people can transform boring conversations into interesting ones, and can make two people perceive that they are closer to one another.

Try taking the opposite side rather than just advocating for your own position. One exercise to build teamwork and open-mindedness is called *Curiosity*. In it, participants form triads where one person, Provocateur, makes a provocative statement on a charged issue such as gun control or gay marriage that is not supported by the one who plays Curious Participant. Curious Participant's role is to ask solely open-ended questions without trying to persuade or influence. The third person, Coach, is an observer and referee. What ensues is a lot of silence and stopping and starting because it is so challenging to explore ideas when we are emotionally invested. Here's an example.

Provocateur: "I believe that all people have the right to bear arms."

Curious Participant: "Don't you care about the mass shootings that occur when guns get into the hands of crazy people?"

Coach: "That was a leading question.   Remember, you mustn't reveal your own position or try to persuade. Try starting your question with 'what' or 'how'."

Curious Participant: "What makes you take that point of view?"

Being curious about the other side of a question levels status in a new way, helping people get over feeling that they are right or better or more enlightened than the people on the other side of an issue. Try this in a meeting with a colleague whose opinion you strongly disagree with. Ask only open-ended questions, and see what happens.

Approach 4: Notice and Express Positive Emotions: Positive emotions can trigger upward spirals, begetting more positive emotion and contagion effects that make groups more creative. Positivity can make people more likely to take positive action. So by increasing positive emotion, you may increase the behaviors that contribute to teamwork.

In one program with 100 client-facing employees at The Westin Savannah Harbor Golf Resort & Spa, we spent time focusing on their individual and collective strengths. All had taken the VIA Survey before the session. They reported that just taking the test changed the way associates interacted with each other and thought about the work that they do.

When they discovered that gratitude was one of their top strengths, a group of employees created a gratitude board. They put it in an employee area of the hotel where associates could post notes for other team members whom they wanted to thank.

In order to care about others in the group, we need to spend time with them. The spa team had significant outcomes in this regard. The spa manager found ways for them to spend more time together. Now they tend to recognize the positive in each other, rather than focus on the negative.

Positive emotions initially arose from taking the VIA survey. These emotions broadened thought patterns and caused people to brainstorm and build the strength of their group as well as empathy towards one another.

All four of these approaches involve forgetting self-interest and thinking about the group as a whole. Put on your director hat, take that 30,000-foot view, and see what happens. The show doesn't go on unless everyone pitches in.

Five Actions to Build Teamwork

by Tayyab Rashid

1. Volunteer weekly for a community service project in your town, one that deals with what you are best at. Find new friends through it who share your passion.

2. Help at least one person yearly to set goals and periodically check on their progress. Offer help and encouragement whenever you think it is needed. If the person wishes to reciprocate, allow them to help you achieve one of your own goals.

3. Play sports for your town or school. Allow the spirit of friendly competition to bring your neighbors closer together.

4. Donate blood or become an organ donor. Encourage neighbors to do the same during shortages.

5. Cook a favorite meal for your neighbor or a friend. Look for times when they particularly need such a favor, such as when they are sick or particularly busy.

All My Sons (Monologue)

by Arthur Miller

Read aloud to explore the strength of teamwork.

Chris: It takes a little time to toss that off. Because they weren't just men. For instance one time it had been raining for several days and this kid came to me, and gave me his last pair of dry socks. Put them in my pocket. That's only a little thing...but...that's the kind of guys I had. They didn't die; they killed themselves for each other. I mean that exactly; a little more selfish and they'd've been here today. And I got an idea—watching them go down. Everything was being destroyed, see, but it seemed to me that one new thing was made. A kind of...responsibility. Man for man. You understand me? — To show that, to bring that on to the earth again like some kind of a monument and everyone would feel it standing there, behind them, and it would make a difference to him. (Pause.) And then I came home and it was incredible. I ... there was no meaning in it here; the whole thing to them was a kind of a –bus accident. I went to work with Dad, and that rat-race again. I felt...what you said...ashamed somehow. Because nobody was changed at all. It seemed to make suckers out of a lot of guys. I felt wrong to be alive, to open the bank-book, to drive the new car, to see the new refrigerator. I mean you can take those things out of a war, but when you drive that car you've got to know that it came out of the love a man can have for a man, you've got to be a little better because of that.

Zest

"Vitality refers to feeling alive, being full of zest, and displaying enthusiasm for any and all activities.... Vitality is zest that is experienced as volitional and fulfilling as it is brought to bear on life's worthy activities."

Vitality "is most noteworthy (and therefore most praiseworthy) when displayed in circumstances that are difficult and potentially draining." CSV-209, CSV-273-275

Recovering Zest and Enthusiasm

by Paula Davis-Laack

Some people wake up feeling tired and depleted. Others are full of energy, ready to take on the day. That ability to feel activated and ready to start the day is not the caffeine in their morning Starbucks calling. It's something deeper. It's the character strength of zest and enthusiasm.

Zest is defined in the VIA character strengths manual as mental and physical vigor. It's about approaching life with vitality, not doing things half-heartedly, and feeling alive.

Fascinating research findings have emerged about the character strength of zest.

Zest, along with the character strengths of hope and teamwork, were more commonly found among American youth than American adults. It seems that zest erodes on the way to adulthood.

All strengths have their own benefits, but people with "heart" strengths such as zest, gratitude, hope, and love find it easier to be satisfied with their lives than people with "head strengths" such as judgment and love of learning.

In a survey of over 9,000 employed adults, zest predicted work satisfaction and whether people viewed their work as a calling.

Unfortunately, too many people today feel just the opposite of zest: tired and burned out.

Several years ago, I was just such a person. I practiced commercial real estate law for seven years, and during the last year of my law practice, I knew something was wrong. I was chronically tired, cranky, and sick. While I was effective in my law practice, as soon as the adrenaline and stress pipeline turned off, my body crashed. I missed more work in the last 12 months of my law practice than I did in my entire working career up to that point. I was also in the emergency room three separate times with digestive issues, and I suffered from panic attacks on a weekly basis. I didn't know that I was experiencing something called burnout.

I now study burnout and its impact on people and organizations. Burnout is generally the absence of zest. One of the three big dimensions of burnout is exhaustion. Burnout is caused by a combination of too many job demands, too few job resources, and not enough recovery from stress. Overwhelming job demands may come from high levels of pressure, an impossible workload, or emotionally demanding interactions with clients and colleagues. Missing resources may include information, autonomy, opportunities to learn new things, a supportive leader, and high-quality relationships with colleagues. Recovery comes from physical activities, hobbies, and time to connect socially with other people.

Understanding what activities rejuvenate you and then actually doing those activities is a critical component of burnout prevention and zest recovery.

I have given the VIA to many different groups of people, from soldiers to human services professionals to lawyers, and I am consistently struck by how few of them have zest as one of their signature character strengths.

When I first took the VIA Strengths Survey in early 2009, zest and enthusiasm ranked near the bottom of my 24 strengths.

That makes sense because I was in the middle of my burnout and completely drained. I dreaded going to work on Monday, and I had unplugged from many of the people and activities that had once given me so much energy. I left my law practice in June 2009, and started my master's degree in positive psychology later that year. As part of an assignment for one of my classes, I had to re-take the VIA. This time, zest and enthusiasm appeared 4th in my list of 24 strengths.

Figure 24: Full of energy

Making the decision to leave my law practice and pursue a career that truly mattered to me helped me re-engage and plug back into what gives me energy and vitality. While you certainly don't have to leave your job to build zest, you do need to understand how much time you're spending on activities that build or drain your energy.

If you're looking to build your zest, try my *Energy Busters and Builders* exercise. Draw a grid with four quadrants. Label them as shown below:

Builds my energy at work: ___ % time spent here	Builds my energy at home: ___ % time spent here
Drains my energy at work: ___ % time spent here	Drains my energy at home: ___ % time spent here

Fill in activities that belong to each square. Once you completed that step, assign percentages to each square. Most people I work with realize that they're spending large amounts of time doing activities that drain their energy, both at home and at work. The goal is to do more things from the first row, the activities that build energy.

The character strength of zest can be an important barometer for how you're doing at work and in life. Companies and individuals would be wise to pay more attention to it.

Five Actions to Build Zest

by Tayyab Rashid

1. Do a physical activity of your choice, one that you don't "have to do" and that you are not told to do. Notice how this affects your energy level.

2. Improve your sleep hygiene by establishing regular sleep time, eating no later than 3-4 hours before sleeping, avoiding doing any work in the bed, not taking caffeine late in the evening, etc. Notice changes in your energy level.

3. Think of ways to make an assignment exciting and engaging before you undertake it. While doing it, see if you can focus to the point where you lose track of time.

4. Watch a sitcom or a comedy film weekly. Invite friends.

5. Do at least one outdoor activity weekly such as hiking, biking, mountain climbing, brisk walking, or jogging, for an hour. Enjoy both the outdoors and your own internal sensations.

What it Takes to be #1 (Speech)

by Vince Lombardi

Read aloud to explore the strength of zest.

Winning is not a sometime thing; it's an all the time thing. You don't win once in a while; you don't do things right once in a while; you do them right all of the time. Winning is a habit.

Every time a football player goes to play, every inch of him has to play.

Some guys play with their heads. You've got to be smart to be number one in any business. But more importantly, you've got to play with your heart.

If you're lucky enough to find a guy with a lot of head and a lot of heart, he's never going to come off the field second.

It is a reality of life that men are competitive. The object is to win fairly, squarely, by the rules - but to win.

I've never known a man worth his salt who in the long run, deep down in his heart, didn't appreciate the grind, the discipline. There is something in men that really yearns for discipline.

I firmly believe that any man's finest hour -- his greatest fulfillment to all he holds dear -- is that moment when he has worked his heart out in a good cause and lies exhausted on the field of battle - victorious.

Complex Character Strengths

by Neal Mayerson

When we set out to create a framework for studying character strengths, we were aiming to develop a taxonomy. We had a retreat in Glasbern, Pennsylvania, at which 20 or so people with diverse professional backgrounds gathered to discuss how to approach this daunting task. One of the professionals had expertise in systematics and informed us that a taxonomy presumes an underlying theory of relationships. Recognizing that such theory did not exist, we were told that our best goal would be to describe a classification, which is in fact what Chris Peterson and Marty Seligman did with the advice and input of a panel of esteemed scholars.

The VIA Classification of Character Strengths aims to identify elemental traits of character, and to organize them conceptually. When confronted with the large array of prospective candidate strengths, Drs. Peterson and Seligman formulated a list of ten inclusion criteria, subjecting each character trait to a rigorous review. The 24 traits that made it into the classification are those that best match the inclusion criteria. Among the aspirations of the classification is to identify elemental positive traits that can combine to form more complex traits, but which cannot be decomposed into one another.

So, the VIA Classification of Character Strengths is like the Periodic Table of Chemical Elements. Hydrogen and oxygen can combine into water, and open-mindedness and fairness can combine into "tolerance." Persistence, open-mindedness, and self-regulation may combine into "patience."

Many people have suggested additional character strengths. For example, John Yeager wrote: "Consummate critical thinking is a rich and complex strength that is comprised of a constellation of many other strengths, including open-mindedness, curiosity, love of learning, persistence, integrity, and self-regulation...

189

Consummate critical thinking is simplicity on the other side of complexity, a constellation of components that are systematically employed to function as the 25th strength of character."

There are many compound strengths of character such as critical thinking, which John Yeager describes so well. However, they do not in fact extend the VIA Classification as he suggests, but do give direction to how compound strengths might be deliberately constructed in efforts to improve the human condition. The VIA Classification of Character Strengths identifies, as best we can, basic elements of character, which in combinations form the rich texture of human character.

This "periodic table of character" offers people a framework for delving into the complexities of this important area of human nature.

Part 2:

Taking Action

Part 2 includes several chapters that explore the question, "Now that we know what the character strengths are, how do we apply this knowledge to make life better for people?"

Scott Asalone and Yee-Ming Tan answer this question in the context of business. Aren Cohen writes about the role that strengths can play on a vacation. Elizabeth Elizardi shows how character strength awareness can enhance life with young children, while John Yeager shows how he used character strengths to work with disadvantaged youth. Finally, Ryan Niemiec explores what research tells us about intentional use of character strengths and how we can put that knowledge to work to improve human well-being.

Cultivating Strengths in Business

by Yee-Ming Tan

Do strengths translate well to workplaces in China? I run positive leadership workshops in Shanghai and Hong Kong, and recently came across an experience in which the strengths-approach was challenged.

"This assessment doesn't tell me my weaknesses, it only contains strengths. I don't get it! What's the point of an assessment that doesn't tell you your weaknesses? How can I improve if I don't know my weaknesses?" Chen shouted from the back of the room. Chen (not his real name) and his colleagues, all highly educated senior managers of a shipping firm, attended my positive leadership workshop in Shanghai two months ago. His colleagues were just as puzzled by the absence of weaknesses in their character strength report.

Chen's top five strengths are fairness, authenticity, kindness, love, and humility. He is confused. There is a dissonance between his reported strengths and his real-life persona. He is known to have a quick temper and regularly fights with his customers. He knows his biggest weakness is the inability to control his temper.

The power of the VIA character strengths is not just in the identification of strengths but in the integration and the shift that comes afterwards. Often a good debrief is required before the individuals can fully make sense of what to do with their strengths. I used the following questions to debrief Chen.

Yee-Ming: How much do you own these strengths (fairness, authenticity, kindness, love, and humility)?

Chen: Definitely fairness, authenticity and humility. But I don't think I am kind, especially not loving.

Yee-Ming: This is interesting. The survey results come from your answers. Let's explore this a bit. In what situations do you display kindness and care? To whom might you show your kindness? We play different roles in life, and we can behave

192

differently in different roles. Perhaps you show more kindness in one role and less in another role?

Chen: That's true. I am kind to my wife and my daughter. I am also like this with my friends. But I am not kind at work. How can I be kind and caring at work? We need to fight for our business. When my client is being unreasonable, I will fight back, unlike my colleagues who are passive.

Yee-Ming: I can see the strengths of fairness and authenticity coming into the picture now. When you sense something is unfair, that is where you might get into arguments with others. Let's try this. How do you behave when you are being kind?

Chen: I'm tolerant, willing to listen to other people, considerate, just like when I am with my daughter. I am patient, willing to listen to her, a lot of give and take.

Yee-Ming: Great. So let's take another step. Take the case of your tendency to argue with your client. If you were to tap into your top five strengths, how could these strengths be applied in such a situation?

Chen: Fairness will ensure that I can always balance the needs of my client and our company position. Yes, I see it now. Instead of getting into arguments that damage the relationship, I can apply my kindness and empathy here. I can be more patient and be willing to listen to my clients. Even if they are wrong, I can show some humility too. In the past, when I sense injustice or unreasonableness, I immediately blow up.

Yee-Ming: Seems like you're found a way to tap into your strengths to deal with a real life situation. Let me know how it works out for you when you are back at work.

Chen emailed me three days later. He had almost started an argument with a client. He remembered to apply his kindness and empathy just before he lost his cool. Because he was able to switch to listening and appreciating his client's perspective, the issue was resolved quickly. He received a big "Thank you!" from the client afterwards.

Chen had been aware of his temper problem, but the traditional deficit-approach had only exacerbated his frustration. He had tried many ways to no avail: learn to be patient, learn to see things from the other person's perspective, suppress his temper, use calming techniques, and so on. He finally succeeded by tapping into his strengths, and did so with minimal effort or exertion of self-control.

People can change most efficiently through who they are to begin with. In Chen's case, his development involved identification of a strength, integration into his view of self, and changed behavior.

As a footnote, I caught up with Chen yesterday. His integration of strengths has helped him turn his former business contacts into friendly relationships. His clients and he are on the same team – not on opposite teams – making his work more fun and meaningful. I asked him to share his insights on the strengths approach, and he said,

"Might as well use them if you've got them!"

Using Strengths Assessments

By Scott Asalone

Organizations from international banking giants to small non-profits are examining the power of strengths focus. I offer day-long strengths workshops to employees and managers and subsequently meet with leaders to embed a strengths-focus.

I'd like to offer some of the best practices I use to get the most out of team discussions as I debrief the VIA.

Start with the positive model of change. Most of you probably already do this. The idea that individuals and organizations move in the direction of that which they focus on is my launching pad for the workshop. Then, I contrast the positive model of change to the deficit model that causes people to focus on problems that need to be fixed. This moves employees toward strengths, but also sets up a later conversation I hold with the leaders about their organization.

Use research selectively. I love research. When I used to love telling everyone about all the research from positive psychology. I've learned a lesson. I use research selectively. Most employees don't care about hearing all the research. A couple of well-chosen studies make the point.

Discuss weakness early. One of the challenges with the strengths instruments is that most people and organizations still focus on weakness. Ignoring weakness or simply commenting that it will go away if you focus on strengths doesn't work. I like Marcus Buckingham's concept that the only weaknesses a person should deal with are their kryptonite (remember Superman). Kryptonite is the weakness that can hinder someone's life or career. Most listeners accept that idea.

Identify the difference between "what" and "how" strengths. Early this year some of the push-back I received over strengths, as identified by the instruments, was that they were not "real." The strengths were not what individuals did each day. Yet

195

after some discussion they realized that the instrument identified _how_ they did things. I now have individuals first write down and discuss with their fellow employees _what_ they do well; their strong tasks and abilities. I then talk about _how_ strengths that can be applied to multiple tasks. By identifying the difference I help employees rearrange their day both with the tasks they do well and how they do their tasks.

Encourage full ownership of strengths. At this point the results from the instrument are still fairly academic. Since most employees in my sessions sit with their friends I have individuals share their results with their friends. Then I encourage the listeners to identify where they've seen the evidence of that employee's strength. Individuals start really owning their strengths when they realize others have observed them.

Acknowledge strengths envy. I've learned not to do a comparison of strengths in an organization because it creates _haves_ and _have nots_. I used to create a matrix of who had what strengths, but employees inquired what strengths the top employees had and wondered how they could develop those strengths. I now acknowledge that some of them might be feeling strengths envy, but show them Tom Rath's comparison of three CEOs who have totally different strengths and note that it is the use of their unique strengths that creates success.

Use strengths. Employees want to know how to use their strengths every day. I have them redesign their entire day as much as possible. They place their _what_ strengths at optimal times during the day as energizers, or rewards for doing difficult tasks. Then I have them identify where their _how_ strengths can make the day or tasks more efficient and more enjoyable. Finally, they either work in dyads with another employee as a coach, or with their entire intact team, to see where they can leverage their strengths even more.

Embed strengths. I believe in action plans. At the end of the day participants create a personal action plan that acknowledges specifically how they will develop their strengths, for example through study, practice, and role-modeling. Then they focus on how they will use their strengths. Sometimes leaders collect the action plans in closed envelopes and returned them to the employee later. Finally I have the entire group brainstorm how they will remind each other to focus on and use strengths.

No matter which approach you use, whether you facilitate this discussion one-on-one or in a larger group setting, you can set the stage for positive individual and organizational change.

Taking Strengths on Vacations

by Aren Cohen

Recently, I took a wonderful vacation with my husband, Andre, to Argentina and Brazil. It was a bit of a last minute trip. I had been working very hard, so I decided that I desperately needed an escape when I had the chance. So less than a month in advance, we booked our tickets and planned our get-away.

While Andre had been to both Buenos Aires and Rio de Janeiro before, I had not. Stylistically, we are somewhat different travelers. I am the sort of person who likes to book hotels and to research sites and restaurants well in advance of a trip so that I know what sort of experiences I am going to have. Andre, who has traveled much more than I have, is comfortable with a "fly by the seat of your pants" approach. Years of experience have taught him that he can always find food and lodging and that sometimes without a strict schedule, the unexpected experiences are more fortunate.

Given that our vacation was planned speedily, it involved a mixture of our planning styles. While we had reservations for our full stay in Rio, we had only one night of four booked in Buenos Aires. Since I had been busy before our departure, I had done only minimal research on sightseeing or dining. However, since Andre had been to both locations before, I decided I would try something new. I happily entrusted myself to him and embraced his "go with the flow" approach to travel. My 10-day trip to South America with my husband provided us both with a tremendous sense of rejuvenation and well-being.

I want to share some thoughts on the VIA Strengths I found amplified on our trip. I will focus on seven:

Curiosity: If there is ever a strength that is related to travel, it is curiosity. Generally when we go to new places, we go with the intention of exploring and discovering. While Andre and I are both able to pursue our curiosities at home thanks to the Internet, it in no way compares with the actual experience of being there. When we travel, our curiosity is fueled with a much greater intensity because everything around us is new and requires investigation. I can look at a picture of Leblon Beach on my screen, but once I am there, I want to experience the water temperature and the taste of coconut milk.

Love of Learning: There was a lot to investigate on our trip, and much of that required my curiosity. However, there were other questions I started asking myself that required more in-depth research, and thus a chance to learn systematically. I was delighted to read plaques in museums that explained what life in the 1800's was like in Argentina, and I quickly set about learning the history of the colonization of Brazil when I got home.

Open-mindedness: Traveling requires open-mindedness. Going to a new place means that you will see things that are done differently and considered in ways that are different from your own. A friend had told me that I should go see Recoleta Cemetery in Buenos Aires. To be honest, I was expecting Recoleta Cemetery to be like Mount Auburn Cemetery in Cambridge, Massachusetts: open, rolling greens, benches secluded under willow trees. Boy, was I wrong! Recoleta is filled with mausoleums stacked more tightly than skyscrapers in Manhattan. It was totally different from what I expected, but it was a chance for me to see how differently Bostonians and Argentineans choose to commemorate death.

Zest: Traveling for pleasure should not be undertaken halfheartedly. Vacations, no matter where you go, should inspire you with a sense of adventure. We ran around Buenos Aires feeling alive and activated, and even when we were on the beach in Rio, there was a palpable energy and excitement. The adventures of vacations allow us to relish and intensify our zest.

Appreciation of beauty and excellence: In Buenos Aires, we went to a couple of museums. In Rio, we spent time on the beach and in a favela. Beauty and excellence can be found

199

wherever you go in all sorts of shapes and forms. In Buenos Aires, the buildings and the art inspired me. Flying to Brazil and looking out the window, I was awestruck by the beauty of the landscape. The best part about a vacation is that the hazy eyeglasses of everyday life are lifted. I do believe that when a person is out of his or her normal routine, it is easier to see the majesty in the world around us.

Gratitude: Vacations provide many reasons to feel gratitude. When we arrived at our second hotel in Buenos Aires only to find out that they only had room for us for one night instead of the three we had thought we had booked, I was not feeling very grateful. However, Andre was very good in that moment of reminding me of his "go with the flow" philosophy. The next night we wound up in another hotel that was even more enjoyable than the one we booked for the previous night. All of a sudden, I found myself grateful for our travel mishap because the unanticipated, unimagined outcome was even better than what we had originally planned. All sorts of little things appear on vacations that elicit gratitude just for the opportunity to experience them.

Yet, at least for me, there is another aspect of gratitude that also comes from traveling. When I hear the airplane captain say, "Prepare for arrival and cross-check," as the plane is landing in my hometown, I swell with gratitude. I love having had the adventure, but the adventure always makes me grateful to be returning to my normal life of home, family, friends, and work.

Love: When you travel with someone you love, the vacation offers opportunities to foster and grow your love. Sharing new and novel experiences together builds memories that become part of your unique intimacy. You grow closer together and seal another bond in the foundation of your relationship, both in the magic of the moment and in the lasting memory it creates.

Cultivating Character Strengths in Young Children

by Elizabeth Elizardi

I was sitting at dinner with my husband and two daughters, ages seven and four, when I was caught in a firestorm of sibling rivalry. Having two very feisty children, what starts out as jovial banter can very quickly descend into mudslinging mayhem without the appropriate channeling and redirection.

In the midst of the battle, one word was uttered that caused the whole table to pause in disbelief: "Stupid." This is one of those words that many parents proclaim is a bad word, a cuss word, a never-to-be-uttered-within-these-walls word. I stole that teachable moment like a bandit and waved it wildly in front of my children. What transpired amidst the redirection was a fascinating discussion about people and their inherent goodness.

I was quick to point out that there is no "stupid" person because every human being is capable of goodness and every human being has something good within. I wanted my children to understand that there are strengths and beauty in all of us. We just have to hunt for the good stuff.

My children were behaving as many of us behave when we are interacting with people in the world. They were pointing out each other's weaknesses, what was wrong, what bothered them about each another, instead of recognizing what is right, good, and strong. How easy it is to slide down that slippery slope of "Stupid."

What character strengths are apparent in children ages three to nine? Nansook Park and Chris Peterson published a study in 2006. In the study, parents wrote descriptions of their children between the ages of 3 and 9 years. The descriptions were analyzed for the presence of the 24 VIA character strengths as well as the children's levels of happiness.

Findings from the study showed that love, zest, and hope were associated with happiness in very young children, and gratitude was associated with happiness among older children. The most common strengths identified by parents were love, kindness, creativity, and humor, while the most uncommon were authenticity, gratitude, modesty, forgiveness, and open–mindedness. Perhaps some strengths require greater maturity to become evident.

Figure 25: Guide a child

While certain character strengths, hope, zest, and love, are strong in all young children, they don't always stay strong.

Given that genetics and environment play a role in developing children's character, how can you identify, cultivate, and support your child's unique constellation of strengths?

Think about how you feel when you are given the freedom to use your strengths and how it feels when other people recognize what is right with you. Wouldn't you want that for your children? But knowing, identifying, and cultivating strengths in young children goes beyond just good feelings. Research shows it has a positive effect on mental and emotional well-being, and it mitigates the risk of anxiety and depression in later years.

Spotting strengths in your children cultivates your appreciation for them and their unique gifts of character. Putting on your strengths lenses enables you to hunt for the good stuff. It helps you avoid thinking that problem areas are permanent and pervasive, keeping you optimistic. Over time, your children will begin to develop an identity or sense of ownership around the strengths, "This is who I am," and "This is what makes me unique and special." You instill the belief that they are competent, confident, and capable of accomplishing their goals. You will become their "persuasive other."

Using strengths creates positive emotions in you and your child, further replenishing the inner wellspring of resources for challenging situations.

You will model an understanding that everyone has potential and everyone possesses some inherent goodness.

If parental documentation is a reliable measure for identifying strengths, where do you begin?

Watch them play. The best way to identify strengths in two or three-year-olds is to observe carefully when they are playing with other children. Listen and do **strengths spotting**.

Reflect on their peak experiences. Were there times you can recall when your children were at their best or in flow? When or where does each child shine?

Ask your children's teachers questions like, "What are their strengths?" and "How would you describe them?"

Expose your children to a wide range of activities, such as dance, music, art, literature, sports, and nature — and not just ones you are prone to enjoy. See if there are any elements within these activities that really light a spark.

Imagine yourself giving a parent-report. How would you answer questions about your children such as "Name your child's strengths," or "What does your child do really well?"

Listen to their stories. Children give us clues about the way they perceive the world in the stories that they tell us. Create the space for conversation and storytelling at dinnertime, in the car, and at bedtime. Listen for strengths in action. Pick up on their clues when they are sharing their day with you and point out the strengths that you hear in their words.

When you plant a new garden, you start with fertile soil. Strengths are fertile soil, and the activities below are seeds that will bloom into a beautiful, lush environment. Here are some ways to keep the garden growing:

Have a **Strengths Dinner**. Let's pretend that one of your child's top strengths is gratitude. Celebrate his/her strength one night by writing a compliment card about how he/she showed gratitude that week and leave it at his/her place setting.

Have discussions about how your child's strengths show up in daily life.

Help your children use their strengths in new ways. Make a list with each child of all the activities he or she can engage in during any given week that would activate top strengths. Keep the lists visible and encourage them to try a new one each day.

Collect comments about each other's strengths. Put a white tablecloth on the dinner table and ask everyone in the family to write on it with fabric marker.

Create situation cards and ask what would you do if?

Do a weekly strengths pick. At dinnertime or bedtime, pick a strength and discuss what it looks and sounds like. Talk about how it showed up in your lives.

Make a **Strengths Wall** in each child's bedroom. Collect artifacts that demonstrate that child's strengths.

Create a **Positive Portfolio**. Get a special wooden box for each child and let them decorate their own boxes. Encourage them to collect artifacts that remind them of their best selves.

Create **Strengths Storybooks**. Paste pictures from real life on blank white paper and draw lines underneath. Help your children write stories about their lives and talk about their strengths.

Share strengths stories in children's literature. Find picture books or chapter books with characters that embody specific strengths and share them with your children.

Identifying and cultivating strengths in young children inspires appreciation for who they are and ignites their senses of possibility.

I find it fitting to close out this article with a song by Red and Kathy Grammer. In it they imagine a world where every child is recognized for his or her unique strengths. That would surely be beautiful.

See Me Beautiful (Song)

by Red and Kathy Grammer

See me beautiful
Look for the best in me
It's what I really am
And all I want to be
It may take some time
It may be hard to find
But see me beautiful
See me beautiful
Each and every day
Could you take a chance
Could you find a way
To see me shining through
In everything I do
And see me beautiful

Cultivating Strengths in High Risk Youth

by John Yeager

I have spent a lot of time helping build strengths among well-adjusted adolescents. Recently, I had the opportunity to work with high risk youth, ages 12-20, who are members of a residential treatment center. These young men grew up in a life of abuse and eventually became violent abusers themselves. At face value, these boys appear to be healthy, but as you hang out with them, you begin to see the pain in their eyes. Each one has already been involved in the department of corrections. As part of their program, they are strictly supervised by counselors. All boys must remain in the sight of a counselor at all times due to impulse control issues. The program provides them with ways to better cope with moment-to-moment living.

All of the boys grew up in an environment that didn't foster trust. They experienced a shame-based climate that has led to immense degrees of guilt and inferiority.

These young people come from unsupportive families, and after being cast away at very young ages, were eventually sent to residential treatment. This is the last stop before jail! They had not had the opportunity to learn effective coping techniques. If your only tool is hammer, you treat everything and everyone else as a nail. This metaphor is, unfortunately, very appropriate.

As part of our three-day program, we brought the boys through a variety of group and individual challenges. These activities were designed to magnify trust, autonomy, initiative, and industry. When we started working on the challenge course (collaborative games and eventually the low and high ropes courses), I observed some of the maladaptive coping techniques coming out in some of their behaviors, but also witnessed bits of trust, initiative, and industry.

After exposure to the ropes challenges, I met with the boys to chat about their signature strengths. Each of them had previously

206

completed the VIA-Youth. It was very interesting to review the individual and collective results to see their signature strengths. The majority of the boys had spirituality as one of their top strengths. Prior to the ropes activities, we took them through our campus, and I could see that several boys were visibly moved by the architecture of the inside of the chapel. This house of worship is a safe haven for many of them. That evening, we discussed how spirituality was a leading strength a majority of them. They remarked that this characteristic comes alive daily for each of them. Later, one young man said that his belief in God is similar to the belayer on the ropes course, always protecting him from falling and other dangers.

The strengths discussion helped the boys know their strengths and see ways that they can express them more often. Knowing what their strengths look like in action can be a valuable addition to their toolbox of life skills.

They then have the cues to pull out the strength when they want or need it. The more that expression of the strength becomes habitual, the greater the odds that that it will be result in healthy behaviors. Being able to name what one does well is empowering. However, this is asking a lot of a young person who been exposed to neglect and abuse.

The strengths that were least endorsed by the group were prudence and humility. They are just starting to develop these strengths through the modeling, dialogue, and consequences process in this program. Humility as a strength is very different from the shame that many of them experienced as they grew up.

The boys were divided into several groups and were instructed to complete graphic representations of their strengths (strength trees). They were provided with a large piece of newsprint-butcher block paper and a variety of markers. The most challenging aspect of the activity was having them try to link their strengths to others in their respective groups. They are at a point in their lives where it is still difficult to see the relationship between the influence their actions have on others, and the ability to trust others to be part of their lives. One boy's appreciation of beauty and excellence came out in a wonderful graphic representation with his group. He was extremely proud of his drawing, and I helped him see how he could use this strength even more in moment-to-moment living.

We noticed in the groups how the overuse of their top strengths could create problems. Another boy, who had leadership as his top strength, was having difficulty motivating his small group to get rolling on their strengths representation. He was getting very frustrated, and I could see the shadow side of his leadership defaulting to biting sarcasm with other group members. With some timely prompting by the residential staff, he gradually got the rest on board, and their final product was quite good. In fact they were the only group to draw strong connections between each other's strengths in the development of a team.

Robert Quinn, the author of *Building the Bridge as You Walk on It*, says, "When we change ourselves, we change how others see us and respond to us. When we change ourselves, we change the world." These young men are re-building their own bridges. With a focus on strengths, they may indeed make it. I hope and pray they do!

Signature Strengths

by Ryan Niemiec

Suppose you want to decide whether someone's strength is a signature strength. If you have only one question to ask, make it:

> "What strengths are most essential to who you are and define you as a person?

This appears to be the single most important criterion in determining whether character strengths are "signature," or not. Other questions such as, "Is the strength energizing?" "Is it easy to use?" and "Is it used across settings?" are important, but are subsumed under this more important question. If you want to get to the heart of the matter, ask about identity.

When I lead workshops, groups, or guest lectures, I have participants take the VIA Survey of strengths prior to the event. I then ask the participants about their experiences with this activity. A 17-year-old adolescent in one of my lectures characterized the importance of one of his signature strengths when he stood up and exclaimed the following:

> *I learned that appreciation of beauty is one of my signature strengths. I never would have framed it that way but that is exactly how I have approached everything in my life. When I'm studying, I try to spend time in nature. When I'm with my friends and they're complaining, I look for the truth in what they're saying – and I see that truth as beautiful. I see beauty in new technologies, old technologies, TV shows, and people. I look for it in colors and patterns, dimensions and sounds. I see things that others seem to walk right on by. It seems to occupy a foreground in my mind and heart as I go about my day. Wonder and awe are always there for me.*

This young man speaks to how his signature strength describes who he is (identity) and also how he approaches life (action). Just so, our signature strengths say something about our positive identity and about the way in which we take action in this world.

Table 1 offers a description of the essence of each character strength and the frequency in which each appears in the top 5 of an individual's profile on the VIA Survey of strengths. While an individual's top 5 are not necessarily all signature strengths, this is a good proxy or starting point.

Research on signature strengths

In the field of positive psychology, one would be hard-pressed to find an intervention with more specific and successful intervention studies than helping people deploy their signature strengths. In a recent study of older adults, signature strengths used in new ways even beat out the other common positive intervention of counting blessings.

This intervention has three steps: take the VIA Survey, identify one of your signature strengths, and use it in a new way each day.

In randomized, controlled trials, this intervention consistently leads to increases in happiness and decreases in depression, sometimes with effects lasting six months.

This exercise has been further validated by revealing benefits across a number of populations, including youth, older adults, employees, people with traumatic brain injuries, suicidal people, as well as in various locations such as China, Australia, UK, USA, Canada, and Europe.

Table 1: VIA strengths and frequency of appearance in respondents' top 5.

Character Strength	Snapshot View	In Top 5
Creativity	Originality that is useful	25%
Curiosity	Exploration/novelty seeking	34%
Judgment	Critical thinking & rationality	33%
Love of Learning	Systematic deepening of knowledge	28%
Perspective	The wider view	13%
Bravery	Facing fears, overcoming adversity	14%
Perseverance	Keep going, overcome all obstacles	17%
Honesty	Being authentic	31%
Zest	Enthusiasm for life	9%
Love	Genuine, reciprocal warmth	33%
Kindness	Doing for others, compassion	32%
Social Intelligence	Insight into what makes others tick	15%
Teamwork	Collaborative, participating in group effort	15%
Fairness	Equal opportunity for all	35%
Leadership	Positively influencing others	14%
Forgiveness	Letting go of hurt, showing mercy	17%
Humility	Achievement does not elevate worth	9%
Prudence	Wise caution	9%
Self-Regulation	Self-management of vices	4%
Appreciation of Beauty & Excellence	Seeing the life behind things	25%
Gratitude	Thankfulness	29%
Hope	Positive expectations/goals	14%
Humor	Offering pleasure/laughter	27%
Spirituality	Connecting with the sacred	19%

Here are a few additional examples of research outcomes specific to signature strengths. For more research results, visit the VIA site at *http://bit.ly/VIAResearch*.

The use of 4 or more signature strengths at work is a cutoff for more positive work experience and work-as-a-calling.

The use of signature strengths is connected with work engagement and work satisfaction.

In many cases, knowing your strengths is not enough. You must use them in your life too.

Character strengths are linked with a better workplace climate.

Character strengths are connected with the various elements of well-being such as engagement, meaning, positive emotions, and positive relationships.

Character strengths are linked with improved achievement and performance.

Character strengths help to buffer stress and improve coping ability.

So how do we translate this research into practice? One woman, a longtime sufferer of depression, was delving into a program on mindfulness and character strengths and was particularly impacted by the character strengths components. Over the decades, she had been a regular customer of psychotherapy and medication to treat her depression. She and I interacted around her several-week practice of "using signature strengths in new ways" with the following exchange:

"I discovered I have to take my *signature strength pill* every day."

"What do you mean?" I asked.

"When I use my curiosity or kindness or gratitude in a novel way, I feel better that day. When I forget to mindfully use a signature strength, I feel worse. It acts like a pill for me."

"Tell me more about that," I replied.

"It's like this – when I take a fresh approach with a signature strength, my ceiling opens up and I see the world more clearly. I see the blueness of the sky and the greenness of the trees. I want to connect with people. I feel better. I'm taking action and I'm taking action with my core parts."

"Sounds a bit like psychological exercise," I observed.

"Exactly, just like running on a treadmill, it keeps me in a healthy place of taking action."

In practice, people may find it challenging to come up with new ways to use their signature strengths. Often we are not well-practiced at using our strengths and when we do use them, we do so without much awareness. For example, have you paid much attention to your use of self-regulation as you brush your teeth? Your level of prudence or kindness while driving? Your humility while at a team meeting?

Practical Tip #1: Anchor signature strengths in new ways with a daily activity.

Choose a regular activity you engage in such as leading a team meeting, handling telephone calls, working one-on-one with clients, walking your dog, talking with someone close to you. Each time you start this activity, say to yourself, "I'd like to bring forth one of my signature strengths in a new way while I'm doing this activity." This will anchor your strengths use into something that is already habitual. New ideas around enhancing strengths will then emerge.

Practical Tip #2: Map one of your signature strengths across the following 4 facets. This will allow you to widen the depth of your view of each strength.

Intrapersonal	Heart
Interpersonal	Mind

Each of the 24 character strengths can be mapped out according these dimensions. Strengths can be expressed through our mind (e.g., logic, analysis, reasoning) or heart (e.g., feeling, body, emotion, intuition) and also behaviorally – interpersonally (i.e., involving others) and intrapersonally (i.e., when alone). Take gratitude as an example. Here's how one client mapped out her gratitude along these facets (this will vary for each person).

Intrapersonal • I can express thanks to my body for its healing capacities. • I am grateful for my connectedness with the universe and want to give back to the environment.	Heart (feelings; body) • Warmth in the chest • Relaxing heaviness in the shoulders • Tingling in the fingers and hands. • Sense of opening up to others and the world.
Interpersonal • Verbally expressing thanks to a friend. • Showing appreciation by offering kindness in return.	Mind (thoughts; beliefs) • My family means the world to me. • I am appreciative of this person's gift. • I am connected to this person.

Practical Tip #3: Be mindful of the following common errors people make around character strengths.

Overfocusing on lower strengths and neglecting top strengths: Lower strengths are important and should be addressed, BUT the core of who a person is should usually be given first priority.

Focusing too much attention on overuse of character strengths, instead of appreciating and celebrating them: Again, overuse is possible with every character strength. For example, it's possible to be too forgiving, as Louisa Jewell pointed out, BUT first things first. Help friends and clients endorse, understand, appreciate, and even celebrate their best qualities first. There is a world of insight that opens up with exploration and use.

Limiting the focus to top 5 only: All 24 strengths matter. While the top 5-7 might matter the most for most people, we all have all 24. Becoming more conscious of how these emerge from moment to moment during a typical day is important.

Jumping to action before understanding: Many people skip the "explore phase" of the aware-explore-apply model of character strengths work. Exploring helps people draw connections to who they are and why this work matters.

Strength mindlessness and autopilot: Forgetting the fact that every person, no matter how self-evolved, has MANY strengths blind spots.

Reflecting and working on character strengths is a life-long process. This is why I view mindfulness as a primary ingredient in character strengths work.

Afterword

We hope you have enjoyed learning the language of character strengths and seeing many ways that they make a positive difference in the world. Curious? This can be the start of an ongoing experience of the beauty of character in the world that surrounds you.

Here are some possible next steps:

Practice: Visit Tayyab Rashid's site at for more ideas for using your strengths in new ways. Remember this exercise is a validated way to increase your own well-being.

http://bit.ly/BuildVIAStrengths

Observe: Watch the people around you. Try to guess the strengths of the people you really care about. Put your observations into words using character strengths language, "I saw you use your creativity there," or "What a great example of open-mindedness." When you are comfortable doing that, try guessing the strengths of the people you have more trouble getting along with. Notice the impact of mindful observation on your thinking about them.

Read: Subscribe to Positive Psychology News where new articles appear several times a month. These articles investigate all aspects of the good life, including character strengths.

http://positivepsychologynews.com/

As you read stories of people in newspapers, novels, or biographies, keep your eyes open for the character strengths that the protagonists display. That will help you grow your ability to spot strengths in others.

As you watch movies or plays, do the same. Ryan Niemiec's book, *Positive Psychology at the Movies, 2nd edition*, is a great place to get started. Since 2009, Ryan has written an annual column for Positive Psychology News nominating the best movies of the year from a positive psychology perspective. Start with the article, which includes links to the reviews for previous years.

http://bit.ly/PPMovieAwards

Read other books on character strengths. *Character Strengths and Virtues* is the encyclopedia on the subject. Ryan Niemiec's book, *Mindfulness & Character Strengths* contains many exercises for building mindfulness and character strengths together. For a review of his book, see

http://bit.ly/MBSPReview

Write: Reflect on your experiences with your own character strengths or those of the people around you. In his outstanding book, *Better,* about ways to do things better, Atul Gawande writes, "By soliciting modest contributions from the many, we have produced a store of collective know-how with far greater power than any individual could have achieved" (p. 256). Think of yourself as a contributor to collective know-how. Consider submitting articles to Positive Psychology News. You can send them to *admin@positivepsychologynews.com*

To keep learning, practice, observe, read, and write.

To your continued growth!

Shannon and Kathryn

Contributor Biographies

In the following biographies, MAPP stands for Master of Applied Positive Psychology. There are now several MAPP programs in the world. The contributors to this book come primarily from the program at the University of Pennsylvania and the one at the University of East London.

Scott Asalone, MAPP, is a speaker, author, minister, teacher, independent bookstore-owner, poet, and entrepreneur. Along with Jan Sparrow, he started A&S Global Management Consulting, Inc. in 1999. Scott has spoken and consulted in Asia, South Asia, across Europe, North America, and Brazil. He has published three books, and currently writes a blog and articles for various online news sources. His passion is achievement and greatness, so he focuses on helping others unleash individual greatness. (Using Strengths Assessments in Business)

Diana Boufford, BSW, RSW, is a social worker employed in private practice and through a hospital in Windsor Ontario Canada. She has been working in psycho-geriatrics for nearly 15 years. She is now working in the hospital's Problem Gambling Service. This gives her opportunities to employ her interest in positive psychology along with her clinical skills in the course of individual, family, and residential counseling around addictions. (Spirituality)

Kathryn Britton, MAPP, is Managing Editor for Positive Psychology News and co-editor of the three books in the Positive Psychology News series. Kathryn is an executive and writing coach. She also teaches Managing Project Teams to graduate project management students at the University of Maryland. Kathryn had 30 years' experience as a professional software engineer, technical leader, and inventor. She co-authored *Smarts and Stamina: The Busy Person's Guide to Health and Performance*, and a chapter in *The European Handbook of*

Positive Psychology. She runs writers' workshops and coaches individual writers. (Book Editor, Curiosity, Humility, Prudence)
http://theano-coaching.com

Aren Cohen, MBA, MAPP, is an educational consultant and learning specialist who uses positive psychology and proven educational philosophy to work with academically, motivationally, and emotionally challenged students. Aren teaches her students to use their strengths of character to change challenges into triumphs. Aren's students are enrolled in a wide variety of the leading schools in New York City. Aren also has a business dealing with beautiful china. (Social Intelligence, Strengths on Vacations)
http://StrengthsforStudents.com
https://facebook.com/TheTalentedTeaCup

Kirsten Cronlund, MAPP, MPOD, is the vice principal of the Bryn Athyn Church School, a private K–8 school in the Philadelphia area. Kirsten also performs in strengths and resilience coaching, helping clients to access the best parts of themselves to overcome challenges and to actualize their goals. She incorporates the findings of individual and organizational flourishing into her leadership style, and she uses cutting-edge research findings to help coaching clients flourish professionally and personally. Kirsten leads workshops and talks on resilience, and she contributed chapters to both of the earlier books in the Positive Psychology News series. (Love and Be Loved)

Paula Davis-Laack, JD, MAPP, formerly a practicing lawyer, is founder of the Davis Laack Stress & Resilience Institute, a practice devoted to helping busy professionals prevent burnout, manage stress, and build resilience. She has taught these skills to thousands of professionals around the world. Her articles on thriving at work appear on her blogs in *The Huffington Post, U.S. News & World Report,* and *Psychology Today.* Her expertise has been featured on *O, The Oprah Magazine,* Fast Company, Forbes.com, *Women's Health,* The Canadian Broadcasting

Corporation, The Steve Harvey TV Show, and Huffington Post Live. (Zest)

John Sean Doyle, JD, MAPP, is a lawyer and poet, and teaches positive psychology at North Carolina State University. Whether writing about work, parenting, home or hardship, Sean's essays are invitations to inject a little more hope, affection and meaning into the world. They are about recovering a reverence for being, and creating a culture of kindness.

http://www.johnseandoyle.com/aboutme

Elizabeth Elizardi, M.Ed., MAPP, is an early childhood administrator and educational consultant specializing in creating strengths-based communities of parents, educators, and leaders who set high priorities on actions that lead to well-being in children. As the Director of Early Childhood at Isidore Newman School, Elizabeth has launched a model program that integrates materials, experiences, interactions, and ideas that promote character strengths and best practices in early childhood education. (Character Strengths in Young Children)

Sherri Fisher, MAPP, M.Ed., is a leader in the field of positive education. An education management consultant, educational coach, workshop facilitator, and author, Sherri uses the POS-EDGE Model, which incorporates research findings from fields like strengths psychology and behavioral economics into positive, personalized, best-practice strategies for learning, parenting, and work. Sherri co-authored the positive education book, *SMART Strengths: Building Character, Resilience and Relationships in Youth*. (Appreciation of Beauty and Excellence)

http://sherrifisher.com/pos-edge-model

Margaret Greenberg, MAPP, spent the first fifteen years of her career in Human Resources, where she consulted, designed, and facilitated sessions for planning, leadership, and team development. Then she founded The Greenberg Group in which she coaches individuals, partnerships, and teams using a strengths-based approach. Margaret co-authored a recent book,

Profit from the Positive. Well-being tools from the book are featured online in the book's online site. (Leadership)
http://thegreenberggroup.org
http://profitfromthepositive.com
Bridget Grenville-Cleave, MBA, MAPP, earned her MAPP degree from the University of East London, UK, where she specialized in the well-being of professional people. Bridget has 20 years' experience in business with a focus on organizational and personal change. Her company, Workmad Ltd, delivers Positive Psychology and Positive Leadership Masterclasses that provide a balance of research and practical tools for personal and professional development. Bridget has authored several books including *Positive Psychology: A Practical Guide.* (Kindness)
http://www.workmad.co.uk
Thomas Heffner, MAPP, is an electrical engineer, human centered designer, and expert in innovation at the Johns Hopkins University Applied Physics Laboratory. He is also one of the founding members of the Design Thinking Corps, with the goal of leading design thinking and innovation across the laboratory. He is passionate about applying design thinking to wicked problems to create revolutionary products, services, and processes that create a better future. (Creativity)
Louisa Jewell, MAPP, is a consultant, facilitator and speaker with over 15 years of experience working with groups on leadership development, employee retention, and team building. Her *Positive Management* workshops promote practices that lead to both higher employee well-being and improved performance. Louisa is the founder and president of the Canadian Positive Psychology Association and is currently writing a book about building confidence. (Forgiveness)
http://louisajewell.com
Homaira Kabir is a women's leadership coach, a cognitive behavioral therapist and an education consultant. She is passionate about empowering women to become leaders of their

own selves in order to become leaders in relationships, at work and in life. Her work with adolescents is focused around helping them harness the brilliance of a key stage in life and shape their paths towards success and well-being. (Humor)

Sandy Lewis, MAPP, is a coach and facilitator supporting individuals, teams, and organizations as they work on increasing purpose, engagement, effectiveness, and productivity. A Senior Human Resources Professional, she has over 20 years of human resources leadership in finance, high tech, biotech, professional services and non-profit firms. Her passion is helping people and teams find their greatness. (Open-Mindedness)

http://positiveshift.us

Neal H. Mayerson, Ph.D., is a clinical psychologist, businessman, and philanthropist. He was in private practice for 15 years treating couples, chronic pain, and eating disorders. As a businessman he developed real estate as well as companies that introduced Purell instant hand sanitizer to the consumer market and personalized, Internet-based health coaching to the healthcare industry. As a philanthropist he has been instrumental in creating non-profit organizations that have served the needs of people with disabilities, abused and neglected children, and teachers. In 2000 he created the non-profit *VIA Institute on Character,* which engaged Martin Seligman and Christopher Peterson to lay the intellectual foundation for advancing the science and practice of character strengths. (Foreword, Complex Character Strengths)

Senia Maymin, MAPP, Ph.D., is the founder of Positive Psychology News, series editor for the Positive Psychology News Series, and coauthor of *Profit from the Positive.* Maymin oversees a network of coaches that specialize in positive psychology methods. She has worked in finance on Wall Street and in technology as cofounder and president of two start-ups. (Series Editor)

http://svchange.com

Ryan Niemiec, Psyd., is Education Director of the VIA Institute on Character. He is also a licensed psychologist, coach, and international presenter. He is an adjunct professor at Xavier University in Cincinnati and the University of Pennsylvania. Ryan is author of *Mindfulness and Character Strengths: A Practical Guide to Flourishing*. He co-authored *Positive Psychology at the Movies*. Ryan created *Mindfulness-Based Strengths Practice* (MBSP), the first, structured program for building character strengths. (Love of Learning, Signature Strengths)

http://ryanniemiec.com

Shannon M. Polly, MAPP, ACC, is a facilitator, speaker, coach, and entrepreneur. Her clients have included Fortune 500 companies and the US Army; and she has lectured at various universities including the University of Pennsylvania, Columbia University, The US Military Academy, and Georgetown University. She is dedicated to developing leaders by combining the science of positive psychology and the art of theater. She partners with clients to leverage their strengths in order to overcome challenges and present themselves powerfully. She studied theater and classical acting at Yale University and the London Academy of Music and Dramatic Art; and she completed the Georgetown Leadership Coaching Program. Shannon is a contributor to the books *Positive Psychology at Work* and *The European Handbook of Positive Psychology*. She is a co-founder of Positive Business DC (@positivebizdc), an organization that inspires leaders to increase well-being, productivity, and profitability in the workplace. (Book Editor, Acting 'As If', Gratitude, Teamwork)

http://shannonpolly.com

Tayyab Rashid, PhD, is a licensed clinical psychologist and researcher at the University of Toronto applying positive clinical psychology, strength-based resilience, posttraumatic growth, multicultural psychotherapy and positive education. Dr. Rashid developed and empirically validated positive psychotherapy (PPT) with Dr. Martin Seligman. He guest edited the special issue of the *Journal of Clinical Psychology* (May 2009) devoted to positive interventions for clinical disorders. Dr. Rashid has trained mental health professionals and educators internationally. He has also worked with trauma victims including the survivors of the 2005 Asian tsunami, 9/11 attacks, and floods in Pakistan. (Five actions to build each strength)

http://tayyabrashid.com

Lisa Sansom, MAPP, MBA, is a credentialed coach and an organizational development consultant at Queen's University in Canada and the owner of LVS Consulting, a boutique consulting firm that helps to build positive organizations. Lisa has been working in organizational development since 2000 at financial, government, education, and health care organizations. Lisa is an active board member of the Canadian Positive Psychology Association. (Bravery)

http://lvsconsulting.com

Jan Stanley, MAPP, is a writer, coach, and former executive. She has worked with Fortune 500 Companies, the U.S. Army, and the Harvard Business School to develop leaders. Jan uses poetry, mindfulness, collaboration, and ritual, woven together into ceremonies of well-being. Jan is a faculty member of the Celebrant Foundation and Institute, where she teaches the beauty and benefits of ceremony. Her short plays have been produced on stage and on television in her hometown, Madison, Wisconsin. (Integrity)

http://habitspracticesandrituals.com

Yee-Ming Tan, MAPP, is an author and executive coach providing leadership training and coaching services to senior executives. Recent clients include Cathay Pacific, Goldman Sachs, Mead Johnson, and Microsoft. She publishes a series of tools, RippleCards, for people who choose to cultivate greater well-being. (Character Strengths in Business)

http://ripplecards.com

Prakriti ("Paki") Tandon, MAPP, was an anchor and producer at CNBC-TV18 in New Delhi, India. Paki has explored the current state of the media through a positive psychology lens. Since the media is a highly influential force on our psyches, she believes we must take great pains to ensure a more balanced combination of positive to negative media. Paki is now working on several projects for the media space to fuse her passion for positive psychology with her talents on camera. (Forgiveness)

Dan Tomasulo, MFA in writing, MAPP, PhD, is a licensed psychologist and psycho-dramatist. He writes for *Psychology Today* as an expert on group therapy. He authors the daily column, *Ask the Therapist*, for PsychCentral.com, as well as their Proof Positive blog on practical applications of positive psychology. He is the creator of Interactive-Behavioral Therapy and the *Dare to be Happy* experiential workshops. His books include *Confessions of a Former Child: A Therapist's Memoir*. He is currently working on a memoir, *The Participants*, about his involvement in deinstitutionalizing the residents of Willowbrook. (Perspective)

http://dare2behappy.com

Douglas B. Turner, MAPP, is the Vice President of Human Resources for the Washington, DC Metro Division of Balfour Beatty Construction. Mr. Turner oversees all aspects of human resources, including leadership, management, employee training and development, team development, employee recruitment and retention, employee relations, and compliance. Mr. Turner also serves as the voluntary leader of a religious congregation with over 400 members. (Hope)

George E. Vaillant, M.D., is a psychoanalyst, research psychiatrist, and pioneer in the study of adult development. He directed Harvard's Study of Adult Development for thirty-five years. He is the author of *Aging Well, The Natural History of Alcoholism, Spiritual Evolution*, and *Triumphs of Experience*. His 1977 book, *Adaptation to Life*, is a classic text on adult development. In June 2009, Joshua Wolf Shenk published an article in the *Atlantic Monthly* entitled "What Makes Us Happy?" which focused on Vaillant's work in the Grant Study, a study of 268 men over many decades. (Love and Be Loved)

Emily vanSonnenberg, MAPP, designed and teaches the UCLA Extension course, *Happiness: Theory, Research, and Application in Positive Psychology.* She has been a researcher for the UCLA Relationship Institute, UCLA Psychology department, and UPenn Positive Psychology Center, and helped teach UC Berkeley's *The Science of Happiness* and UCLA's *Human Motivation.* Emily consults for government and private organizations, and operates a private practice to help people cultivate meaningful and fulfilling lives. Through articles and speaking engagements, Emily translates psychological research into a digestible language offering practical guidance and well-being strategies for the general public. (Self-regulation)
http://psychpositive.org

John M. Yeager, Ed.D., MAPP, is Director of the Center for Character Excellence at The Culver Academies in Culver, Indiana. John consults with schools on the inclusion of character education in academic, leadership, and athletic programs. He is the co-author of *Character and Coaching: Building Virtue in Athletic Programs,* the sole author of *Our Game: The Character & Culture of Lacrosse,* and a contributor to *Gratitude: How to Appreciate Life's Gifts.* John's most recent book is *SMART Strengths.* (Character Strengths of High-Risk Youth)

Emiliya Zhivotovskaya, MAPP, founded the Certification in Positive Psychology (CAPP) program now located in 6 cities in the United States with over 200 graduates. Emiliya is the founder of The Flourishing Center dedicated to the flourishing of individuals, organizations, and communities around the world. Emiliya is on the faculty at Saybrook University where she is pursuing her Ph.D. in Mind-Body Medicine. (Persistence)
http://certificateinpositivepsychology.com

Credits

Haresh R. Makwana for the cover design.

Jane Kenyon for "Otherwise" from *Collected Poems of Jane Kenyon*. Copyright @2015 by The Estate of Jane Kenyon. Reprinted with the permission of The Permissions Company, Inc. on behalf of Graywolf Press, Minneapolis, Minnesota, (*http://www.graywolfpress.org*).

Debbie Swick for the photograph of Christopher Peterson from the first World Congress of the International Positive Psychology Association.

David Kelley and Douglas Dietz for the creativity story about reinventing MRI machines to stop scaring small children. For the full story told by Douglas Dietz himself, see his 2012 TEDx talk called *Transforming Healthcare for Children and Their Families (http://bit.ly/DougDietzTEDx).*

Excerpt from *A Raisin in the Sun* by Lorraine Hansberry, copyright © 1958 by Robert Nemiroff, as an unpublished work. Copyright © 1959, 1966, 1984 by Robert Nemiroff. Copyright renewed 1986, 1987 by Robert Nemiroff. Used by permission of Random House, and imprint and division of Penguin Random House LLC. All rights reserved.

See Me Beautiful from the recording, Teaching Peace
©1986 Smilin' Atcha Music
Written by Kathy and Red Grammer
Distributed through Red Note Records
http://www.redgrammer.com

Tayyab Rashid for permission to use selected items from *Building Your Strengths (http://bit.ly/BuildVIAStrengths).*

Acknowledgments

Shannon thanks...

My mother, Linda Nolan Polly. Your writing put my father through medical school, and you encouraged me to write. Sending the poems I wrote at an early age to magazines taught me perseverance. Thank you for editing this book with an eagle eye.

Senia Maymin and Kathryn Britton for your wisdom in creating Positive Psychology News Daily and conceiving of this book series.

Kathryn Britton for your appreciation of beauty and excellence, grit, and countless hours of work as we brought this book to life together.

Cathy Salit, David Nackman and Maureen Kelly at *Performance of a Lifetime* for your inspiration and introduction to the work of Vygotsky.

Angie Flynn-McIver for introducing me to the opening monologue from *Chesapeake*.

Garry Reeder for your patience, perspective, and wisdom.

Quinn and Harper Polly-Reeder for teaching me about zest, prudence, bravery, kindness, gratitude and love.

Kathryn thanks...

Shannon Polly for making sure we didn't drop the ball, for style and creativity, and for teaching me what I've gained from years of reading aloud to my children and husband.

Edward Britton for supporting me in too many ways to name.

Karen Long for being my sounding board and friend.

Thomas Britton, Laura Britton, and Jedediah Purdy for being part of my world. Each of you shows a unique and fascinating combination of character strengths. Indeed, there are many more than 24 ways that people can be strong.

Together we thank...

Kevin Gillespie for the beautiful, original drawings. Thank you for your skill and patience. You transformed vague ideas into evocative images.

All the contributing authors listed on page vii for your gracious willingness to contribute to this project in memory of Chris Peterson. Your support and encouragement kept us going.

Matthew Polly for a thorough, hard-headed, sometimes biting, sometimes applauding, but always good-humored review.

James Pawelski for help with the William James passage.

Steven Leifer, Angus Skinner, Kat Koppett, and Chris Ringer for suggestions and assistance along the way.

Andrea Allmayer and James Pawelski for their assistance in establishing the Christopher Peterson Memorial Fellowship.

Martin Seligman and Neal Mayerson for your visionary work on character strengths.